CAMERON TAYLC   ' ated from Aberdeen U.. cisity in 1979
with a degree .. ....,, and had a career in tne Civil Service
before returning to his native Orkney to become CEO of Orkney
Tourist Board. He established Seabridge Consultants in 2000 and
has pursued a variety of cultural heritage and tourism interests
since then. Now living in Moray where Macbeth's ghost still
haunts the past, his first book, *Rooted in Scotland*, was published
by Luath Press in 2007.

ALISTAIR MURRAY established Atlantic Marketing in 2004 after a
varied career spanning three continents and ranging from oil exploration to running manufacturing and media companies. He pursues a
number of interests in the creative industries and undertakes strategic
consultancy from his Caithness base, in the far north of Scotland,
where surging Atlantic tides wash the jagged edge of Europe.

On the Trail of
The Real Macbeth,
King of Alba

CAMERON TAYLOR
and
ALISTAIR MURRAY

Luath Press Limited

EDINBURGH

www.luath.co.uk

First published 2008

ISBN (10): 1-906307-31-8
ISBN (13): 978-1-906307-31-8

The paper used in this book is recyclable. It is made
from low chlorine pulps produced in a low energy, low emission
manner from renewable forests.

Printed and bound by The Charlesworth Group, Wakefield

Typeset in 10.5pt Sabon
by 3btype.com

Pont's Map of Elgin and northeast Moray reproduced by permission
of the Trustees of the National Library of Scotland.

All other maps by Jim Lewis

Contents

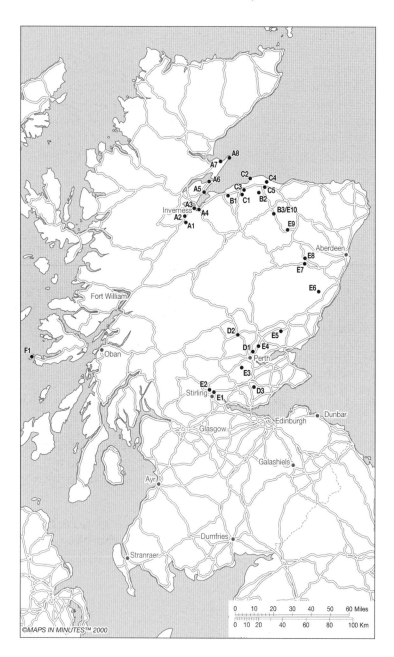

Key to Map

THE STORY WE have told in *On the Trail of the Real Macbeth* takes you to a number of locations in the landscape where important events relating to Macbeth actually or possibly took place. These locations are listed below with brief story notes. The map references are marked in the text where the places are mentioned, Ordnance Survey grid references are included and the page number where the location is first introduced is included in brackets.

CHAPTER I

A1 Dores Beach (NH 597 349), at the northern end of Loch Ness; a view Macbeth would have been acquainted with and where we begin our story (p25)

A2 Old Bona Church (NH 602 385), on the Caledonian Canal; next to an old fording place on the River Ness in Macbeth's day (p28)

A3 Inverness Museum (NH 666 451), in the centre of the city (p28)

A4 Auldcastle Road (NH 674 456), supposed site of Findláech and Macbeth's fort in the Inverness area (p29)

A5 Rosemarkie (NH 737 576), an attractive small Black Isle town; location of a church believed to date from the fifth century and where Macbeth may have passed fleeing from Moray in 1020 (p34)

A6 Cromarty (NH 785 677), another small and historic Black Isle town; location of a ferry across to the Tarbat Ness peninsula, possibly where Macbeth caught a small boat into Viking lands in 1020 (p35)

A7   Portmahomack (NH 914 840), sited on the Tarbat Ness peninsula; location of a modern Pictish visitor centre and where, in 1020, Macbeth may have sought temporary sanctuary at a monastery (p35)

A8   Tarbat Ness Lighthouse (NH 945 872), stunning site with views across the Moray Firth to Moray, where Macbeth may have vowed to return to Moray before catching a ship south to Malcolm II in 1020 (p36)

CHAPTER 2

B1   Auldearn (NH 917 556), site of a medieval castle and the probable location of a fortified residence in Macbeth's time; where he possibly surrounded and burned Gilla Comgáin and his war band to death in 1031 (p47)

B2   Birnie (NJ 206 587), site of an early church; potentially the location where Macbeth and Gruoch married in 1033 (p47)

B3   Mortlach (NJ 323 392), site of a monastery and church in Macbeth's time; The town is now called Dufftown; located on the eastern boundary of Moray (p47)

CHAPTER 3

C1   Cluny Hill (NJ 043 590), probable site of one of Macbeth's fortified residences; possibly where Macbeth received news of Duncan's accession in 1034 (p53)

C2   Burghead (NJ 108 692), ancient Pictish fort; perhaps where Macbeth would have stood to gain best advantage looking across to the battle of Torfness in 1035 (p58)

C3   Sueno's Stone (NJ 046 595), ancient carved standing stone; where Macbeth may have mustered his troops in 1040 before enjoining Duncan in battle (p63)

C4 Pitgaveny (NJ 226 658), just to the north east of Elgin; where Macbeth is believed to have defeated Duncan in battle in 1040 (p64)

C5 Elgin Cathedral (NJ 221 630), now ruined; this did not exist in Macbeth's time but is alleged to be where Duncan died after fighting with Macbeth in 1040 (p65)

CHAPTER 4

D1 Scone Moot Hill (NO 114 266), next to modern Perth; the location where 10th and 11th century Kings of Alba were inaugurated, including Macbeth in 1040 (p69)

D2 Dunkeld Cathedral (NO 023 426), did not exist in Macbeth's time; ancient religious site where St Columba's relics were brought for safety in 843; the power base of Abbot Crinan (p73)

D3 Loch Leven (NT 159 989), site of a Culdee community in Macbeth's time; Macbeth and Gruoch gave grants of land to the Culdee community here (p81)

CHAPTER 6

E1 Logie Church, Bridge of Allan (NS 815 969); site of a church in Macbeth's time and a vantage point where Macbeth could have watched Norman knights crossing over swampy ground north of modern Stirling to enter the heartlands of Alba in 1053 (p109)

E2 Darn Walk (NS 788 976), old pathway along the River Allan; where Macbeth could have led any visitors across to Dunblane in 1053 (p110)

E3 Forteviot, near Dunning (NO 052 175); the site of Kenneth MacAlpin's wooden palace and possible where Macbeth had a fortified residence (p111)

E4 Dunsinane Hill, near Collace (NO 212 316); where Macbeth is thought to have met Malcolm Canmore and Siward of Northumbria at the Battle of the Seven Sleepers in 1054 (p114)

E5 Glamis Castle, near Forfar (NO 385 480); childhood home of HRH Queen Elizabeth the Queen Mother and mentioned in Shakespeare's Macbeth. There is no evidence of the real Macbeth here but it is close to the edge of the Mounth (p117)

E6 Cairn o'Mount, near Fettercairn (NO 650 805); at the edge of a major trail over the Mounth, where Macbeth may have led raiding parties into Angus between 1055 and 1057 (p118)

E7 Kincardine O'Neil, Aberdeenshire (NO 590 997); where Malcolm Canmore probably passed on his way north chasing Macbeth in 1057 (p118)

E8 Lumphanan, Aberdeenshire (NJ 576 037); the emotive location where Macbeth met his death in 1057 at the hands of Malcolm Canmore (p118)

E9 Mossat, near Essie (NJ 476 195); where Lulach was supposedly lured to his death by Malcolm Canmore in 1058 (p119)

E10 Mortlach (NJ 323 392), on the border of Macbeth's Moray; from where Lulach probably left the safety of Moray to meet with Malcolm Canmore at Essie in 1058 (p121)

F1 Iona (NM 287 244), an historic island off the west coast of Scotland; where Scottish kings, including Macbeth, are buried (p121)

Foreword

Macbethad mac Findláech, more widely known as Macbeth, persists as one of Scotland's iconic stories. King of Alba after slaying Duncan, his was a path to power later mirrored by the supreme warrior King Robert Bruce and the murder of Comyn. Back-projecting from the present has made Macbeth one of the great 'we' stories in Scotland's history. And oft have the Scots thought fit to remind the world, and themselves, of who they are. Credit here the English playwright from Avon: not in any factual sense, of course, since the three witches must rival Walter Scott's spider for Bruce as the ultimate of fabrications. But he created a grown up story for a grown up nation, 'The Scottish Play' no less. Credit the historians who right his inventions while *Macbeth* continues to shoehorn Scotland into world culture, from homage to *The Simpsons* in *MacHomer* (1996) to facing down Italy (*Othello*), Denmark (*Hamlet*), and England (*King Lear*) in *Shakespeare's World Cup* (2002). All together now, 'We're on the march wi' Alba's Army …'.

On the Trail of the Real Macbeth is a tour through the Scottish psyche, and our authors take us deep into this turbulent world. No tourist track here, but an essential visit to the 'foreign country' that is our past. For sure this takes us into a Scotland of the imagination and the many Scotlands to be found along the way. Our authors dissect one of the nation's signature monarchs, a kingship recast by future needs. The paucity of evidence and the literary and political embellishments from later generations are as big a double-edged sword for the historian as Macbeth himself may have used to gain his throne. What follows is your guide. Thumb it well as you travel through your past.

Professor Graeme Morton
University of Guelph

Shakespeare and Macbeth:
Fact versus Fiction

WILLIAM SHAKESPEARE was the finest of dramatists but he did the real Macbeth no favours. Just look at some of the inaccuracies.

Shakespeare says...	History tells us...
Macbeth was an upstart who usurped the kingship	Macbeth had a legitimate claim to the kingship
Lady Macbeth was ambitious and scheming, and goaded her husband to regicide	Lady Macbeth was Gruoch. She was of Royal blood but we know nothing of her character. She and Macbeth were married for 24 years
Banquo was the ancestor of the Stewart succession to the throne of Scotland	There is no record of Banquo in Macbeth's 11th century world
Macbeth murdered the sleeping King Duncan whilst the latter was a guest in his castle	Macbeth defeated Duncan in open battle for the kingship of Alba
Macbeth ruled for a short time, perhaps no longer than 10 weeks	Macbeth ruled Alba for 17 years providing strong and capable leadership
Macbeth was killed by MacDuff at a battle near Dunsinane following an invasion of Alba by Earl Siward of Northumbria	Macbeth was defeated by Siward and Malcolm Canmore (Duncan's son) following an invasion, but continued to rule for three more years

Read on and learn more about the real Macbeth, King of Alba.

Preface and Acknowledgements

WE FIRST BEGAN trying to unravel the story of the real Macbeth as part of a tourism, heritage and technology competition sponsored by Highlands and Islands Enterprise. The aim of the competition was to demonstrate how the use of technology could bring so-called heritage tourism to life.

Our entry for the competition was based on telling part of the story of Macbeth's life and times in Moray, using a variety of different media including a distributed audio story that people could listen to on their mobile phones while visiting three of the locations connected with Macbeth. We were lucky enough to win the competition.

The King Macbeth web site www.kingmacbeth.com allowed us to engage with a wider audience but there seemed so much more we wanted to know about the real Macbeth, King of Alba. And so we began work on this book. In it we tell King Macbeth's story using what little evidence exists for 11th century Alba, in an effort to bring this fascinating man – who ruled Alba for 17 years – to life. In order to make sense of the narrative we found it essential to visit the actual places where the events in Macbeth's life took place, or may have taken place, so as well as Macbeth's story you will find a detailed touring itinerary at the back of this book. It will help you to escape from the main tourist routes and explore a different world. We hope that you will use it, as we did, to follow in King Macbeth's footsteps.

Gavin MacDougall of Luath Press Ltd, our publisher, was encouraging and supportive from the outset and his team has been patient and helpful throughout. We are very grateful to them all.

Everyone we met during our research has helped us – from the charming information assistant in the tourist office in Perth to the farmer's wife who pointed out the rough location of Lulach's Stone while counselling against any attempt to wade through an ocean of mud to reach it. Graeme Morton, Professor of Scottish Studies at the University of Guelph, kindly read through the manuscript and pointed out the most glaring errors. If he was surprised to be asked to read a book that crosses the boundaries of travel guide, history and drama he was kind enough not to complain. Any errors or eccentricities of interpretation that remain in the book are of course entirely our own.

Our respective families have been patient and sympathetic through this voyage of discovery that took us on adventures through blizzards and floods, as well as prolonged periods of research and writing. The final acknowledgement, however, must be of William Shakespeare's genius. We may disagree with the monstrous caricature he made of King Macbeth but the fact remains that without his famous tragedy *Macbeth*, the real Macbeth, King of Alba would lie in relative obscurity.

Figure 1: Alba
(Map showing Alba; Moray; Vikings; Cumbria; Northumbria.)

Introduction

NINE AND A HALF centuries ago, Mac Bethad mac Findláech – the man we know today simply as Macbeth – stood on the windswept summit of Dunsinane Hill and looked out over the fertile heartlands of the Kingdom of Alba. He saw fields and scattered houses; he saw the river Tay in the distance and, looking further, the hills of the Lothians; to the north he saw the mountains of the Mounth[1] with his homeland of Moray beyond; and he saw an approaching force, come to challenge his right to be King of Alba.

Perhaps, as William Shakespeare would have us believe, the sight of the advancing spearmen really did make it seem as if Birnam Wood had come to Dunsinane. Did Macbeth have any inkling of his future – in life or in legend – when he looked out from the fort perched on Dunsinane Hill's one thousand foot high summit?

Shakespeare's Macbeth is an iconic character and probably the best known in the English language. While many people have heard of Shakespeare's Macbeth, few know that he was a real person and fewer still know much about the actual story of his life. There are only a few precious documentary records of Macbeth's time but plenty of subsequent myth-making.

Early chroniclers such as John of Fordun and Andrew of Wyntoun began the process of historical myth-making, continued then by Hector Boece and Ralph Holinshed. Shakespeare was reliant on the works of these earlier writers whose writings would not be classified as history by today's standards. The recounting of myth as fact and the fabrication of new 'facts' makes it abundantly clear why it is sometimes said that history is created, not discovered.

But William Shakespeare too must shoulder some responsibility, for while he may have had to rely on the imperfect testimony of his predecessors, his famous play – the so-called Scottish Play, so unlucky its name must not be spoken in theatres – created new myths alongside others long perpetuated. In just the same way as Hollywood does today, Shakespeare created a piece of work for entertainment. In doing so he used the historical Macbeth for his own purposes – to flatter a royal patron and entertain his audience.

The bard's imaginary creation, a real man made fiction, seems almost to have taken on a life of its own. The real Macbeth would not have recognised his alter ego; or perhaps he would have recognised him, and mocked him. Beyond Shakespeare too, there are new interpretations and modern myths alongside some inspired new creations. Opera, film, television and now the media of the digital age have all sought inspiration in the myth or the man that was Macbeth.

This layer upon layer of myth and misrepresented or misunderstood half-truth alongside the authentic story gives modern scholars the almost impossible challenge of interpreting the past. With so little evidence to go on there are no absolutes, only possibilities and probabilities, evidence examined in ever finer detail to settle academic arguments. These scholarly challenges confronted us in writing this book. Should we take sides when debate became difficult, or should we seek a middle way and tell a believable story, leaving others to continue the arguments? We have chosen to tell a story that we believe to be true but we have shown the sources of our ideas (see the numbered references in the text and the corresponding notes in Appendix A) and included a list of selected further reading.

Given the paucity of documentary evidence, even the chronology of events is open to dispute. The chronology that we have used as the framework for the story that unfolds in the book is included as an appendix with some notes.

Finding the real Macbeth, King of Alba, is a trail that takes us on a journey into the geography and history of Scotland. Macbeth was not the monstrous caricature created by William Shakespeare; he was a real man who was born in the Province of Moray in the early years of the 11th century. Moray was a powerful and independent-minded part of the Kingdom of Alba, a kingdom that in time was to become today's Scotland.

Climactic, dynamic change was taking place throughout Europe, shaping the continent's future and Alba was subject to these same influences. This was the age of the Viking ascendancy in the north of Europe, the birth of feudalism, the rise to power of the Roman Church and schism with the east.

The story of the real Macbeth is every bit as compelling as Shakespeare's fictional drama, perhaps even more so. *On the trail of the real Macbeth, King of Alba* uses the available evidence to try and place Macbeth's story in the actual landscapes where the events of this fascinating period occurred. It tells Macbeth's story alongside a detailed touring itinerary that will enable you to come with us and visit the places associated with Macbeth as we explore his life and times.

This was a very different world to ours but it is where we came from, and the characters in our story are people we would recognise today despite the passing of some 30 generations. Their language was different, their experiences, values and expectations too, but these are the people of Alba.

Mac Bethad mac Findláech, Son of Life, son of Findláech, bids you welcome to his story.

Early Life

IMAGINING THE PAST

When writing *On the trail of the real Macbeth, King of Alba* we found it useful to include a short imaginative piece in each of the chapters as a way of making Macbeth's story come alive. Here is the first of them. Look for the others at the start or end of each subsequent chapter.

The young man was tall for 15, fair haired and red cheeked with just a hint of stubble on his chin. Having collected the tribute from the small farm above the loch his eyes were now fixed on the forest below. Spying movement, he ordered his men to release the dogs and the chase began. The hounds forged on, crashing through the undergrowth. After a while the barking was followed by silence. Quickening pace, the pursuers tumbled onto a small beach. There, Macbeth caught his breath and watched a deer swimming frantically away from the shoreline. Then the dogs closed in and killed their quarry.

CHAPTER I

Early Life

THE BEACH IN QUESTION is not at the very end of Loch Ness, but it feels like it. A thousand years ago it probably sat on the edge of the province of Moray where Macbeth was born around 1005. It is highly likely that he was acquainted with this vantage point and his view would have been much the same as ours, except perhaps for a wooden fort or look-out post occupying the striking location where Urquhart Castle's later ruins now lie to the south west. No houses existed then at the water's mouth, where today the village of Dores nestles around the small bay.

Standing here (A1) the majesty of the Great Glen is overwhelming. Its faulted sides rise steeply 1,000 feet above the famous body of water where St Columba commanded a local monster to *go no further* in 565 whilst saving a local's life. This ancient valley has been used by men as a route way since the great ice sheets vanished, but links to the past are often obscured. Such is the case with Macbeth's 11th century realm, a world that shared some similarities with ours, but which in other ways was very different.

11th Century Alba

The north of Britain at this time contained five different ethnic groups. Macbeth's world was Alba, the 11th century Celtic kingdom that formed the heart of what we know today as Scotland. Though its core is taken to be the area between the Forth and the Spey and east of the mountains of the Highland massif, the borders of Alba were uncertain, changing as power shifted between its rivals to the north, west and south. Internally, rival dynasties ruled over semi independent provinces. The Kingdom of Alba had emerged around 900 from the unification of the Picts and the Scots. The

Figure 2: Map of ethnic groups
(Picts; Britons; Angles; Scots; Vikings)

Britons and Angles in the immediate south took a little longer to become part of the emerging country whilst the Vikings in the west and north never became part of Alba though, as we will see, they played a part in its history. Much further south, Vikings and Saxons vied for control of what would become England.

A thousand years after Christ the whole of Western Europe was in the midst of a transition period. Its peoples, bounded by cultural and behavioural norms, had no way of knowing how dramatic the resulting changes would be. Some scholars have even termed this period the one in which Europe finally emerged from the Dark Ages and it is true that historical facts from the 11th century are not very numerous. But, what we do know is that in 1020, when our story begins, Macbeth was of royal blood. He was the son of Findláech, who was the ruler, Lord or Mormaer, of Moray, arguably the most turbulent province of Alba.

Macbeth's World

So what was this world of Macbeth's like? Well, let's begin our journey by heading north to Inverness where Macbeth's father would have kept a residence. In a car from Dores today you can reach Inverness in just over 10 minutes. In Macbeth's time the majority of people would have walked. This may be a sobering thought for modern travellers but a brisk hike from the beach at Loch Ness would get you to Inverness in two hours; a moderate walking pace would get you there in three. If you were physically able to travel back through time and walk in the 11th century itself then perhaps the first thing you'd notice was the quiet. With the noise of the 21st century absent, apart from human and animal sounds, only church bells, anvils or the din of clashing weapons would have carried across the landscape.

The climate of the 11th century was at least as warm, if not warmer, than our own conditions. Tree cover would have probably spread across a wider area climbing further up the hillsides than it does today. There would have been limited roads or tracks and only a few bridges at strategic river crossings. It is highly likely that there were no bridges at all in Moray and rivers would have been crossed at fording points. One of these was situated two miles into our journey, where the Old Bona Church stands next to the river Ness at Kirkton (A2). Located across the river on the site of an earlier church, the view today of the modern Caledonian Canal is hidden by trees, much as it probably was in Macbeth's time.

We can imagine that many conversations might have taken place at this meeting point, although most of us wouldn't have understood what was being said. In the British Isles in 1020 three Celtic tongues were probably still in use. These were Gaelic, Pictish British and Welsh (or Cumbric) British. They co-existed with Old Norse, Old English and Latin, the latter tongue acting as the glue for the flourishing Christian Church[2].

It's a fair bet that Gaelic had reached Inverness from the south west sometime in the 100 years before Macbeth was born. In his time there may have been a few residual pockets of Pictish British speakers in the province of Moray but we will assume that Macbeth spoke Gaelic. Given the proximity to the Viking lands of the north, perhaps he was also able to converse in Old Norse.

Inverness 1020

Inverness today is a bustling English speaking community with a modern castle standing proud over the river Ness and looking down on a crowded city centre built up over a late medieval town. Inside Inverness Museum (A3) there is archaeological evidence of major dwelling sites, such as Culduthel and Craig Phadraig, which existed in the area from Iron Age times onwards. When Macbeth lived here the setting was a strategic junction for people travelling north, south, east or west.

A cardinal spot such as this, also providing access to sea routes, is bound to have had some sort of 11th century fortification. No one knows exactly where this might have been, but there are clues. According to local folklore the area around Auldcastle Road (A4), on high ground just to the east of the city centre, is the alleged location of one of the residences of Macbeth's father, Findláech. Although you can reach here by car, climbing up a steep embankment path gives you a better sense of scale. At the top there is a natural viewpoint that looks out across an industrial landscape. Beyond this, the large Kessock Bridge marks the entrance of the river Ness into the Moray Firth.

Travel by water was easier in the 11th century for the transport of both materials and people and a landing place would have been located close by. It starts to makes sense as you stand here that a fort existed on this spot. It guarded both land and sea approaches and was a difficult locality for a surprise attack. What may surprise you is that the sea level in the 11th century was probably slightly higher in relation to certain parts of the Moray Firth coastline than it is today. This meant that back then, in the immediate vicinity of Findláech's fort, the flatlands below the steep slope would have been salt marshes.

Imagine standing there as Macbeth would have done as a young man. Picture the 11th century scene. Sweeping to the east beyond the first headland are the heartlands of Moray. Across the narrow Firth are the lands of Ross. In Macbeth's time these would have been reached either by boat or by travelling west towards modern day Beauly around the water's edge. Some people have alleged that Macbeth's family came from this area[3], termed the Black Isle, or at least they ruled there before gaining power in Moray.

Macbeth's Pedigree

Macbeth's father Findláech was the son of Ruadri. Ruadri had another son called Máel Brigte who had been Mormaer of Moray before Findláech and who was killed in battle with Vikings sometime between 985 and 995. Before his death Máel Brigte fathered two sons, Malcolm and Gilla Comgáin, nephews to Findláech. Contemporary Irish sources[4] claim that Findláech was King of Moray rather than Mormaer. Whatever title was used we know very little about Findláech apart from his own battles with northern Vikings sometime between 995 and 1014. We assume here that as a war leader Findláech ruled the Moray area as Mormaer.

The line of kings of Alba itself might be thought of as unusual today in that sons did not normally follow fathers to the kingship. This was shared by collateral royal lines where brothers or cousins were most likely named as heirs before the reigning king died, a practice known as tanistry. This may simply have evolved because two discrete power groups were not strong enough to cancel each other out, and so they ended up having to share the kingship in turn. Whatever the origin, what was essential was that the most vigorous male who could protect territories, and who was suitably connected to the bloodline in the male line, held sway. In this brutal society kings, more often than not, met unnatural deaths.

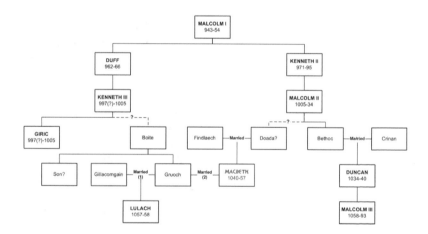

Figure 3: Macbeth's Royal Connections

Some sources claim that Moray's 'royal line' came from the Cenél Loairn kindred group, or clan, who centuries before had produced some of the Dalriadan kings on the west coast, and who supposedly entered Moray through the Great Glen. Others surmise that Findláech may even have been part of the royal bloodline of Aed, son of Kenneth MacAlpin himself, and a descendant of the rival Cenél Gabran kindred of Dalriada[5]. Whatever the truth, we know that from 900 all the Kings of Alba had either come from Aed's line or that of his brother, Constantine I. In 1020 Constantine's direct descendant Malcolm II was ruler of Alba. Although the Mormaership of Moray may have been a royal appointment in the distant past, by the time of Macbeth's father it is assumed to have been a hereditary position with allegiance owed to the King of Alba.

A Celtic Society

Ruling in Moray, Findláech operated through an extended family and household comprising of his war band, poets, clerics or administrators, and servants. This household would have moved around the area rather than staying in one place. This meant that as well as having a fortified residence somewhere in the Inverness area Findláech would also have used a number of other secure houses, essentially large farmsteads, within the region. These would normally be located within a day's travel of each other and, by moving from place to place, the Mormaer could be both visible and accessible in this very Celtic land where respect and power were all important.

Historically, leaders of Celtic societies were originally rulers of people as opposed to rulers of distinct geographical areas. It has been suggested by some[6] that a tribal and travelling culture, combined with a propensity for fighting both inside and outside the tribe, was one of the reasons that a major European Celtic empire never evolved. An echo of this can be found in the war band that travelled around with the Mormaer of Moray.

The war band consisted of a group of personal retainers or

bodyguards[7]. It most likely would have been composed of local, high social status members although, perhaps, suitable incomers may have been admitted to the fold at times. Kitted out with weapons and horses this group would have been the social elite of 11th century Moray, forming a basic military unit organised for war on a permanent basis. What bound a war band together was the legitimate and personal power of the leading male.

The size of any war band reflected the status, power and success of its leader in being able to provide food. The productive capacity of the home area was therefore vital, bolstered by distributable assets, or patronage, gained from raids outside the home territory. In Moray, Findláech's war band might have comprised of anything between 30 to 100 individuals. Members of this band not only pledged their allegiance to, and fought for a leader, but they lived and slept together in great wooden halls. Privacy as we know it simply didn't exist. At night this heroic society would retell great stories huddled around a fire, such as tales of their ancestors or reminiscences about their own exploits.

An Enigmatic Past

Sources of evidence for most 11th century activities are extremely scant. Some *annal* records exist that were contemporary, but these are bare and were often written outside Alba. There are also some examples of contemporary poetry from which we can get an impression of what it might have been like, for example, to fight in a battle. Then there are later *sagas* and *chronicles*, albeit some of these appear to be more mythic than factual. On top of all of this, once you factor in the probability that medieval scribes, working in different languages and often through word of mouth, might copy down the wrong names or dates, then a veritable detective agency is required to peer back through the mists of time.

A number of sources allude to the fact that Macbeth's mother was of royal blood, but only one source[8] mentions her name, Doada. It implies she was a daughter of Malcolm II, King of Alba itself.

Although the source is not contemporary, we think that this would have made sense in a world where to influence the wellbeing of a kingdom leaders would have to identify other key individuals, and then use these networks to make deals. Treaties between adjacent powerbases were often sealed with royal marriage alliances and if Doada was a daughter of Malcom II, then Macbeth would have been a grandson of the King of Alba. We assume that this was, indeed, the case.

Fight or Flee

During Macbeth's early life he would have been groomed for leadership. Although this situation mirrors examples from our own age there were fundamental differences. Men in the 11th century counted on their physical strength in terms of being able to work on and maintain farms and being able to fight. Violence was never far from the surface and any son of royalty would have spent much time learning the art of war and the power of intimidation, presumably through real raiding parties as well as hunting. Learning to administer justice from his father or foster father, solving problems and understanding how to influence kin groups would all have made sense to the young Macbeth.

This acute awareness of how his world worked presumably stood him in good stead in 1020 when, possibly on return to Inverness from his hunting escapade, Macbeth learned that his father Findláech had been slain by his cousins, Malcolm and Gilla Comgáin[9]. We have no related details to hand, but this would almost certainly have been an internal dispute for the leadership of Moray and it ran entirely consistent with the collateral form of rule.

Just imagine that your father has been killed by a close relative. What would you do? In the 11th century one immediate answer would have been to leave the area for reasons of personal safety. Macbeth might have tried to go to his grandfather, Malcolm II, in the heartlands of Alba to the south. Heading there overland would have been a dangerous journey, perhaps through unfamiliar territories.

If a quick decision had to be made then it would have been easier to head north. This was a dangerous buffer zone between Moray and the northern Viking dominions. But it was close by and it may have been a landscape that Macbeth knew well.

The Black Isle

Following the trail across the Kessock Bridge we enter the territory of Ross on the Black Isle, a place in later centuries associated with witchcraft. The landscape feels old, being part of the extended Moray Firth basin area where the rich earth has been colonised by farmers since very early times. It is not inconceivable that farmers in the 11th century may have organised their lives not too unlike those of crofters today. The farming may have been good but for generations Picts, Scots and Vikings all strived for domination before the Kingdom of Alba emerged.

Amidst this tempestuous panorama early 11th century society was organised along the lines of extended families. Then, the custom was for land to be passed on by inheritance. In practice this most likely meant that new generations had to divide up the ownership and so parcels of land probably got progressively smaller. This dynamic would often force some of the younger males away from the home farm to look for more opportunities elsewhere. This invariably spelt trouble for someone else.

The control of productive land was the basis of political power and warlords wielded power through their resident war bands. The majority of the population farmed the land. Many were virtual slaves, though perhaps not in the oppressive sense that the modern usage of the word 'slave' implies, and most of those that were free were poor. For those born into the wrong family there was, more often than not, probably not much to enjoy. Pagan customs that were close to nature sat side by side with the Christian religion in a world where magic and the afterlife were very real. Perhaps people shared the same hopes and fears at Rosemarkie (A5) as we do today, where a church is believed to have developed as early as the fifth century.

Some later historical sources[10] imply that Macbeth was the Thane of Ross. A Thanage can be thought of as the next noble tier down from a Mormaer. However, the term was probably not widespread in Scotland until the 12th century and we have no way of really knowing if Macbeth did have influence here. If so, it would probably have been with one eye always looking to the north. Travelling again in that direction we arrive at the port of Cromarty (A6). A likely landing place In Macbeth's time, if he had looked across the narrow entrance to the Cromarty Firth, he would have been close enough to almost touch the lands of the Vikings.

The Viking North

First recorded raiding around the shores of Britain in 793, by Macbeth's time the Vikings were no longer occasional attackers. They had settled large areas of the north and west as well as in Ireland and in parts of England. Their ambitions were a political threat to Alba. Moray and Ross were on the front line, facing first Sutherland, then Caithness and Orkney beyond. As time passed intermarriage meant that the Vikings were not an alien, distant people. Thorfinn the Mighty, another grandson of Malcolm II of Alba, became Earl of Orkney in 1014 following his father Sigurd's death at the battle of Clontarf near Dublin. Thorfinn was thus a cousin to Macbeth, but they were sometimes rivals in later life.

Just across the water from Cromarty lies the Tarbat Peninsula. This finger of land reaches out into the Moray Firth and, in older times, was a terminus for trade and cultural exchange. Following the small back roads it doesn't take long to reach the visitor centre at Portmahomack (A7). This sits on the site of an old church and monastery that some say was founded in the 6th century. Certainly, by the 8th century it had developed into an important political and industrial complex within the land of the Picts, the original inhabitants of northern Scotland.

Shortly after 800 the monastery was attacked by Vikings, but then remained active until later times. If Macbeth had reached here in 1020 the area would have been nominally under the control of his cousin Thorfinn. But, even today, the Pictish legacy on the peninsula is visually strong, marked by elaborately carved standing stones. Some think that these were posted to prevent ancient mariners foundering on the rocky shores. We will never know for sure, though near a modern lighthouse (A8) there is a stunning view that explains, better than 1,000 words, how close these northern kingdoms were to each other in Macbeth's time.

What Next?

Macbeth may have stood on Tarbat Ness looking back over the sea to the plain of Moray wondering how to reclaim his birthright. Why would Macbeth have done this? Well, we said earlier that some-one of royal blood in the 11th century would have been groomed for leadership. If we also add to Macbeth ambition, ability and a desire to avenge a murdered father, then the die is cast.

Here, there would have been ample opportunity for Macbeth to catch a boat to take him directly to his grandfather, Malcolm II, King of Alba, probably somewhere around Tayside. If Macbeth had been fostered out to his grandfather at an earlier age, which is not inconceivable, then he would have known what to expect.

With no sons of his own that we know of, Malcolm II lived in an era when the succession arrangements for European kings were beginning to change. For instance, within four years of Macbeth's flight, in 1024, Conrad II was elected ruler of the Germans by common agreement, but with only a slight claim to the kingship. This came from the female, rather than the normal male, side.

Three years later, in 1027, one of the guests at Conrad's inauguration ceremony was Canute. Here was a mighty king who ruled over a domain including England and parts of Scandinavia, a true North Sea empire. We know that in 1031, on his return to Britain, Canute headed north to gain the submission of three 'kings' identified by some as Malcolm II, Echmarcach and Macbeth. For Macbeth to be present at this meeting meant that during his sojourn away from Moray he had achieved a high status. But what had actually happened to Macbeth in the decade following his flight from home, and what build up of events had brought the mighty Canute to Alba?

The Winning of Moray and Gruoch

IMAGINING THE PAST

King Malcolm watched the three boys as they listened to the storyteller, their attention focused on the warp and weft of imagery and meaning he wove as he told them tales of their ancestors. Malcolm had heard the tales before many times but the storyteller was a good one and the King nodded in satisfaction.

There remained a difficult problem. Macbeth, Thorfinn, Duncan: the future of Alba. But which one of them was it to be?

CHAPTER 2

The Winning of Moray and Gruoch

IN 1020 THE YOUNG Macbeth – probably only 15 years old – was forced to come to terms with the murder of his father at the hands of his cousins. Historians might describe these times dispassionately as the Moray succession being decided in the traditional way, by violence. But just imagine how Macbeth must have felt when he heard the news.

Our story puts him at Inverness at the time and then Tarbat shortly thereafter before heading south to the household of his grandfather, Malcolm II. As we have implied, it's likely that Malcolm had fostered Macbeth when he was younger. Fostering of young men in the households of relatives would have been a common enough occurrence at all levels of society but it was especially significant in royal households. As the next generation of leaders, in this way young men would have gained maturity and experience away from their maternal home and had the opportunity to create the networks of friends – and enemies – which they would either benefit from or suffer from in later life.

Malcolm would not only have welcomed back his grandson, he would have gained an option for future political bargaining.

King Malcolm II

Malcolm II had come to the throne of Alba in 1005, the year of Macbeth's birth. Opinions about his reign differ with some seeing it as strong and successful; others characterising it as a period of difficulty and weakness. His reputation, certainly, is not that of a gentle man. Kingly perhaps, but not necessarily kindly. The historian Richard Oram captures the sense of the matter when he describes him as 'the master practitioner of single-minded ruthlessness',[11] pointing to his nicknames 'The Aggressor' and 'The Destroyer'.

Malcolm had slain his rivals to win the throne and then, as so many new rulers did before and after, he embarked on a raid into northern England. New kings had to demonstrate their leadership qualities and martial prowess to their new subjects, and also get the measure of the leading men of their kingdom. Armed struggle tested bonds of friendship and loyalty in a very real way.

Malcolm's expedition of 1006 took him to the defences of Durham, a place of religious and political significance where the new king would have sought a victory to consolidate his hold on power. Instead he was routed.

Clearly he recovered from this early setback because he ruled Alba for a further 28 years. We can imagine him retiring to Alba to lick his wounds, rebuild his forces and secure alliances to protect his power. It was doubtless to do the latter that he married one of his daughters to Earl Sigurd of Orkney, a powerful potential rival in the north.

Thorfinn Sigurdsson

One child of this marriage was Thorfinn, a young man whose later life became entwined with that of Macbeth, not least because he too was fostered at the court of his grandfather. Thorfinn was probably born in 1009 and it seems that he was fostered with Malcolm before Sigurd departed for Ireland in 1014, carrying with him a magical raven banner.

The story of Earl Sigurd's infamous raven banner is told in the *Orkneyinga Saga, the History of the Earls of Orkney*. This later Icelandic compilation of oral tales recounts how Sigurd was given a magical banner by his mother, a sorceress. The banner guaranteed him victory in battle but also the certain death of the standard bearer. At the Battle of Clontarf near Dublin in 1014 Sigurd's banner was unfurled and carried into battle but each standard bearer in turn was killed before victory was assured. Eventually Sigurd ran out of willing heroes and, in frustration, wrapped the standard around his own body and entered the fray. True to its design the banner assured victory but Sigurd did not survive to see it.

Given Thorfinn's presence at court the death of Sigurd gave the boy's grandfather Malcolm II tremendous leverage in the north, even though the Earldom of Orkney and Shetland was initially split between Thorfinn's half-brothers. Some historians interpret the situation as one in which the young Thorfinn became ruler of Caithness and Sutherland, firmly under Malcolm's wing, while his half brothers divided the heart of the earldom between them. Perhaps this was the case.

Friends and Rivals

Macbeth would have been nine years old in 1014, old enough to pay attention to the stories told about the great battle at Clontarf. In fact, if he had already arrived at Malcolm's court by then, he and Thorfinn may have listened to the stories together, perhaps both entranced by the memorable tale of the magical raven banner. This was an age of oral tradition, where a lot of knowledge was transmitted from person to person and generation to generation by the telling of stories. Society was shaped by the storytellers, Alba's memory.

Interpretation of later events suggests that Thorfinn and Macbeth were rivals and, given the way that power was exercised in the 11th century, the two boys would have expected this to be so whatever their youthful friendship may have been. Rivalry in youth would have served to hone their skills but their relationship is unlikely to have been one based on bitterness or hatred: things just were as they were and the boys will have had respect for each other if not affection.

There is a third young man who features strongly in the events of the next chapter in Macbeth's life: Duncan, son of Abbot Crinan of Dunkeld and his wife Bethoc. Bethoc was Malcolm II's daughter so Duncan, born around 1002, was another grandson of King Malcolm.

There is an intriguing possibility that the three young men – Macbeth, Thorfinn and Duncan – were all fostered in the King's household at the same time and our belief is that they knew each other well from that special apprenticeship.

We do not know what responsibilities young Macbeth was given in Malcolm's household. We can imagine that he was kept busy, if for no other reasons than to keep his mind off his father's murder and in order to vent the natural energies of a teenage boy. He would have hunted, developing leadership skills and he would doubtless have been taught the arts of warfare – courage, resourcefulness and decisiveness. All qualities he would need, and more, in later life. As he gained in confidence and maturity he would have become of more use than burden to the King, and Malcolm was not without need of resourceful men for he had ambitions for Alba and dangerous enemies abroad.

King Canute and the Empire of the north

One of Malcolm's most dangerous neighbours was King Canute, ruler of a northern empire that included England, Denmark, Norway and parts of Sweden. Born in Denmark, Canute was the son of Sweyn Forkbeard and grandson of Harald Bluetooth. Sweyn had become the King of Denmark on the death of his father and subsequently gained additional lands and power when he became ruler of most of Norway. His wider imperial ambitions included the conquest of England and in 1013 Sweyn led a Scandinavian force that included Canute to England and conquered. Sweyn's sudden death soon after this initial success led to the withdrawal of the force until a new army, this time led by Canute himself, invaded again in 1015. At the end of a fierce and bloody campaign Canute emerged in 1016 as the King of England.

Succeeding his brother as King of Denmark in 1018 and adding the throne of Norway and part of Sweden in 1028, Canute's empire was even bigger than his father's and he became a major figure in northern European politics until his death in 1035.

Malcolm II of Alba will have watched events unfold in England with interest and doubtless a little concern. Canute was emerging rapidly as a powerful and ambitious rival, though the strength of his hold over his English territories, especially the northern ones, must have seemed open to challenge.

The Battle of Carham and the expansion of Alba

Malcolm II found it impossible to resist the temptation and in 1018[12], in alliance with Owain, King of Strathclyde, he invaded Northumbria where he defeated a Northumbrian force led by Earl Uhtred at Carham-on-Tweed on the present Anglo-Scottish border. Lothian, north of the Tweed, was ceded to the King of Alba and the defeated Uhtred was assassinated on the orders of a doubtlessly furious King Canute, well aware that Malcolm had seized an opportunity for conquest before Canute had consolidated his power in England.

But Malcolm's victory also brought an unexpected bonus in that Owain of Strathclyde appears to have died soon after the battle, most likely of his wounds, and Malcolm probably took the opportunity to absorb Strathclyde into the Kingdom of the Scots.

We do not know whether the young Macbeth, aged 13 in 1018, witnessed the battle of Carham but he must at the very least have listened rapt to the stories told of the victory of his grandfather and his followers and allies. Malcolm II's prestige – that all important quality – must have been at its highest throughout Alba and beyond. He had enlarged his kingdom and, some would have said, successfully challenged the King of England. But Alba and Canute had unfinished business. Canute had yet to build his northern empire and so was not the powerful leader he was to become.

For now, though, Malcolm could concentrate on consolidating his hold over the enlarged Kingdom of Alba.

Meanwhile in Moray

Our chapter opened in 1020 with the grieving Macbeth taking refuge at the royal court following the murder of his father Findláech. The *Annals of Ulster* record that '*Findláech son of Ruaidri, King of Alba, was killed by his own people*' and the *Annals of Tigernach* report that '*Findláech son of Ruaidri, mormaer of Moreb [Moray], was killed by the sons of his brother Máel Brigte.*'[13]

The description of Findláech in one of the chronicles as 'King of Alba' has led some historians, including Woolf, to suggest that the Moray dynasty may actually have challenged Malcolm for the kingship. This would have meant that Moray considered itself a separate kingdom to Alba. Without more evidence we will never know whether this was actually the case and our assumption here is that Moray was a *Mormaerdom*, subject to Malcolm II, albeit, as we suggested in Chapter 1, operated in a semi-independent manner.

The sons of Findláech's brother Máel Brigte – and therefore cousins of Macbeth – were Gilla Comgáin and Malcolm. Malcolm became Mormaer of Moray, presumably in 1020 following the death of Findláech, and nothing is known of his rule until the chronicles record his death – probably of natural causes – in 1029. Gilla Comgáin then became Mormaer and we can imagine Macbeth, now 24 and with years of experience at court and in battle behind him and an acute awareness of the tradition of alternating succession, being absolutely furious at the news. It is possible that King Malcolm II supported Macbeth's claim to the Mormaership of Moray and may even have declared him Mormaer in opposition to Gilla Comgáin's assumption of the role.

We do not know a great deal about Gilla Comgáin but the little we do know is of great importance to the story of Macbeth. Gilla Comgáin had a wife called Gruoch, daughter of Boite, who in turn was the son of Kenneth III. Kenneth III had ruled Alba between about 997 and 1005 until he was defeated and killed by his cousin Malcolm, who then became King of Alba. This is a tangled web that would not be out of place in a modern soap opera but the important thing to note is that Gruoch was therefore a royal princess (probably from Fife) with a claim to the throne of Alba. And she and Gilla Comgáin had a son Lulach, a male claimant to the kingship.

King Malcolm must have been uneasy about the marriage and doubly so about the birth of Lulach, consequently perhaps his support for Macbeth's opposition to Gilla Comgáin's Mormaership of Moray is not so unlikely. But before either Macbeth or Malcolm could exert their will in Moray there were more pressing problems to attend to. King Canute had not forgotten the events at Carham in 1018 and his gaze was turning to Alba once again.

Canute moves north

There is – almost inevitably – some debate about the date of Canute's invasion of Alba but 1031 seems most likely. What drew him north at this time? Most likely it was a combination of factors – Malcolm II's apparent support for some of Canute's Scandinavian opponents; opportunism in the light of growing internal unrest in Alba; or perhaps a sense of unfinished business. Canute went on a pilgrimage to Rome at about this time, the act of a man perhaps making his peace with his God in the knowledge that the time had come to put his affairs in order.

Whatever the reason for the invasion, one version of the *Anglo Saxon Chronicle* records that '*In this year* [1031] *King Canute went to Rome and as soon as he came home he went to Scotland, and the Scots king surrendered to him...*'[14] It is thought that the invasion reached as far as the Tay, right into the heart of Alba. Malcolm was forced to submit to Canute, albeit the description in the chronicle reveals the true nature of the submission '*... and became his man, but he observed it but little time.*' Intriguingly, one version of the chronicle refers to the submission of three 'kings', Malcolm and two others. There has been a great deal of scholarly debate about the identity of these two other individuals[15] and there is a strong likelihood that they were Macbeth and Echmarcach. The latter – probably a sub-king in the west of Alba – need not concern us here, but what was Macbeth doing in 1031 and why might he be described as a 'king'?

Macbeth was 26 years old in 1031 and he may have been Malcolm II's war leader, a leading general and therefore of sufficiently high status to accompany the King when he submitted to Canute. Or alternatively Macbeth had, as some historians believe, been named Mormaer of Moray by Malcolm in opposition to Gilla Comgáin and, given the symbolism of the action, the King wanted it to be known that he was important enough to accompany him when he met Canute. We can only speculate. We can speculate too, though, that a meeting with such a powerful figure as Canute had a profound impact on Macbeth. Was Canute a role model for Macbeth, firing his ambition still further? Perhaps Macbeth's own pilgrimage to Rome later in his life was an echo of the awe he must have felt at meeting the charismatic Canute.

Having accepted the submission of King Malcolm and his companions Canute left Alba. He must have known, as Malcolm knew, that the submission was hardly a sincere one likely to lead to a fundamental change in relations between Alba and the empire of Canute. Malcolm submitted because he had no choice, not because he wanted to.

Crisis in Moray

It seems that Macbeth decided that the time had come to act at last. The *Annals of Ulster* record under the year 1032 that, '*Gilla Comgáin, Máel Brigte's son, the mormaer of Moray, was burned, along with 50 of his men.*' We can suppose that at the very least this was done in Macbeth's name but the likelihood is that Macbeth himself was responsible. Killing in this way is a common theme in the Icelandic sagas and medieval Alba would have been no different. The killing involved surrounding a building and barricading the occupants inside before setting it alight. Any victims who escaped the flames were killed by sword or spear.

There was no dishonour in killing opponents in this way. It

made for rapid and complete regime change with little collateral damage and it is likely that Gilla Comgáin's entire war band perished with him. We can be fairly sure that the killing took place in Moray, but the precise location is not known. Perhaps we can imagine it was a fortified building on top of the raised mound in the village of Auldearn (B1), on which King William the Lion was to build a castle more than 100 years later[16]. If it was, Macbeth could have stood beside the smoking ruins of the building and looked out across the Moray Firth towards Tarbat Ness where he had stood grieving 12 years before. Now, Macbeth had won Moray and avenged his father.

Not everyone connected with Gilla Comgáin was killed in the fire, however. Gilla Comgáin's wife Gruoch and their son Lulach had survived the fire or were elsewhere at the time. Macbeth married Gruoch, perhaps in 1033. This simple statement begs so many questions. Did they already know each other? Was this a political match or a love match, or both? How did Gruoch feel about the killing of her husband? How did Lulach feel about it, and did Macbeth feel sympathy for a young man now left in the same position that he himself had been?

And what of Malcolm II? If he supported Macbeth in order to get rid of a potential rival for the throne of Alba he must have been furious when Macbeth married Gruoch, offering protection to Lulach and creating a stronger personal claim to the throne. We might speculate that when in 1033 Malcolm ordered the killing of Gruoch's nephew, the last claimant to the throne in direct male descent from Kenneth III, it was an act of rage and spite.

The chronicles do not tell us where Macbeth and Gruoch's marriage took place. It is likely that it took place at one of the Celtic churches that existed in Moray at the time. Neither history nor archaeology can help us too much here. The two earliest Celtic Christian sites are at Birnie (B2) and Mortlach (B3) in modern Dufftown. Birnie, near Elgin, may have been where the marriage took place given its proximity to Macbeth's Moray heartland.

The first Celtic church and monastic settlement at Birnie was established by St Brendan 'the Navigator' in the early sixth century.

There is no visible trace of this earliest settlement but the site at Birnie, set on a circular raised mound, is deeply evocative. There is a Pictish stone in the kirkyard, testament to the site's age, and the distinctive Celtic bell in the existing church building is believed to have been used since St Brendan's day. The bell was ancient in Macbeth's day and it is possible – just – that it was rung to mark the marriage of Macbeth and Gruoch at Birnie.

Reflecting its ancient importance Birnie was the first recorded seat of the Bishop of Moray from 1107 to 1115 and the existing church building dates from around 1140. It is recognised as one of the oldest church buildings in continuous use in Scotland.

Wherever Macbeth actually got married – and Birnie is a likely candidate – he and Gruoch would have had little time to celebrate. The basis of power was wealth and wealth came from the land: Macbeth and Gruoch had a province to manage.

Land and people

The economic basis of 11th century Alba was agriculture: the produce of the land. Agriculture was geared to the production of surpluses that could sustain a growing population and provide sufficient wealth for King, Mormaer and church.

11th-century society was almost entirely rural-based and agricultural, probably organised along the lines of the extended families or kinship groups that characterised Celtic society. This was not a world where individualism and the nuclear family were the norm; survival depended on the wider kinship group. Settlements were dispersed across landscapes that had been the subject of forest clearance for generations, though there was still plenty of forest in which to hunt.

The agriculture of the time was a mix of pastoral and arable, the latter not carried out in an intensive way. The lack of sufficient quantities of fertiliser meant that arable fields had to be left fallow to recover rather than being continuously used. The limited knowledge of more modern, sophisticated crop rotation techniques meant that management of the landscape was more measured and less demanding of the soil than modern intensive farming practices. Only half the available land would have been cultivated each year; the other half left fallow to rest and recover from the previous year's growing season.

The principal grain grown on arable land was bere (a primitive form of barley), oats and rye. Though now almost completely replaced by other crops, bere has been grown in Scotland since pre-historic times. Today it is grown principally in Shetland, Orkney and the Western Isles where it is tolerant of the cool temperatures and short growing season.

Control of productive land was the basis of political power so the rich farmlands of Moray underpinned the province's independence and importance. The same was true throughout Alba. As you follow the trail of Macbeth on the ground you will see that all the fortified sites dominate good agricultural land but at the same time were dependant on it. Power and land were inextricably linked.

Two kinds of rents were paid. Firstly, people who held land from the Mormaer or other landholders had an obligation to provide hospitality. Mormaers were itinerant, therefore, travelling around their lands and receiving – and consuming – tribute. At the same time they made themselves visible as leaders and were able to dispense justice quite literally at first hand.

The second type of rent was surpluses that were gathered at storehouses for later collection or consumption. These would most likely have been fortified places, if for no other reason than to keep animals out. Surplus produce collected in this way could be traded for goods that could not be produced locally.

The first Scottish coins date from the reign of King David I (1124–1153), in other words 100 years after Macbeth's reign. Prior to David I's reign there were few coins in Scotland though some Anglo Saxon coins have been found.

In the absence of coinage, cattle would have been almost a form of currency in 11th-century Alba. Certainly they were a source and an expression of wealth. Although the balance changes over time and varies geographically, about half the total livestock were cattle, with the rest being sheep and pigs. Pigs could be left to forage, especially in woodland, but cattle and sheep needed reasonable quality arable lands.

Bartering and payment in kind would have been the main form of exchange and tribute would have been paid in kind rather than in cash. In many ways this made for a simpler, more stable economy, firmly tied into the relationships between people as members of the same society and established order.

We have no way of calculating an accurate figure for the population of Alba in the 11th century. Estimates for the population of Scotland in 1300 range from 500,000 to 1,000,000 so a reasonable guess for Macbeth's time might be between 300,000 and 500,000, spread in extended family groups in small communities or 'touns' scattered across an agricultural landscape.

Much like the rest of Alba, Macbeth's home territory of Moray was a landscape of scattered pastoral and arable agriculture, un-cleared forest and marginal lands unsuitable for the simple farming techniques of the time. Population pressures were not forcing the wholesale clearance of forests and farming was not intensive, so any blasted heaths inhabited by Shakespeare's imaginary witches would doubtless have been natural rather than man-made.

In Moray, most settlement would have been inland, away from the sand dunes and estuary silts along the province's long coastline. But not too far inland, for farming would become harder in the higher ground towards the south and the mountains. The richest farmland, and therefore the most valuable, is known today as the Laich of Moray and this is likely to be where the highest status settlements were located, dispersed across the landscape.

An Alban Succession Crisis

As they travelled through their province together, Macbeth remembering childhood places and Gruoch coming to terms with the momentous changes in the life of herself and her son Lulach, much of their talk must have been of events elsewhere. Against all convention, somewhere between their boyhood and manhood Malcolm had weighed up his three grandsons – Macbeth, Thorfinn and Duncan – and chosen Duncan, who turned out to be weakest, to succeed him as King. Malcolm may have regarded Duncan as the most legitimate heir but the King's reputation for ruthlessness suggests that the strict letter of law and convention was not always uppermost in his calculations. Whatever his reasons may have been, the die was cast.

Alba was in the grip of an impending succession crisis.

Everything Depends On This

IMAGING THE PAST

The Mormaer of Moray sat quietly inside the great hall composing his thoughts. His men waited patiently, grouped around their leader. Presently, a flurry of noise from the doorway signalled to Macbeth that it was time. Turning proudly he greeted the messenger. As the news unfolded everyone looked at Macbeth with apprehension. His expression didn't flinch, ordering hospitality for the man who had brought the momentous tidings. Only in Macbeth's head were there thoughts of foreboding.

CHAPTER 3

Everything Depends on This

THE NEWS WAS bleak indeed. Malcolm II was dead and his grandson Duncan was to be the new King of Alba. This inauguration, which actually took place on 30 November 1034, required the support of the ruling elite. The fact that it happened only five days after Malcolm II had passed away reflects the necessity of the age to forestall potential trouble. It is highly likely there would have been anxiety in certain quarters to ensure a smooth succession from potential challengers, such as Macbeth and Thorfinn.

We can also speculate that Macbeth himself would have appreciated the political manoeuvring required for Duncan to become King at Scone, the place where all Kings of Alba were appointed. If Macbeth had sat in his wooden hall on top of Cluny Hill (C1), in the very centre of Moray, he may have remembered life further south. He had of course tasted it before, meeting and interacting with powerful men at the court of Alba, before travelling north to claim his Mormaership. Was he now jealous? Duncan's ceremony at Scone was many days overland from Moray, though not so far by boat, and Macbeth had been the old king's grandson too. The Mormaer of Moray had a valid claim to the kingship, and his marriage to Gruoch gave him another.

Once installed as King, Duncan would immediately assume the potent legitimacy of the position. At least in the short term that is. The balance of power was ever changing, and whether the current change would be for the good or the bad would now depend on the mettle of the new leader. If Macbeth entertained rueful thoughts the only thing that mattered now was anticipating Duncan's actions. Clues might come from his background. So where did this new King of the Scots, Macbeth's cousin, hail from?

The Dunkeld Connection

We have seen already that Duncan was the son of Malcolm II's daughter Bethoc. She had married the powerful Crinan, Abbot of Dunkeld. In a world where power was all, Crinan may well have been an Abbot. However, in all likelihood he would have also ruled the area around Dunkeld, possibly as a Mormaer. This is the area we know today as Atholl.

Crinan's specific pedigree is disputed by some historians but we are fairly sure that he fathered a half brother to Duncan called Maldred, who married into Northumbrian royalty. When Duncan himself came of age, as befitting his high rank, he was given an area to rule by his grandfather. This was the south west part of Scotland.

In the first half of the 11th century the south west would have been peopled by an ethnic mix of Britons, Celts and Angles, with a fair sprinkling of Viking settlers. Whether or not the ancient British Kingdom of Strathclyde was still in existence, who ruled in the area around Galloway, and what the specific extent of Duncan's early geographical power base actually was is unknown. But Duncan's first title may have been King of Cumbria.

It appears that Duncan was Malcolm II's chosen heir. Why, we don't know. Perhaps it was the proximity of the powerful Dunkeld power block, or perhaps Bethoc was a favoured daughter? Whatever the truth, the significance of Duncan's accession is that he became the first King of Alba to succeed in the direct line, as opposed to being from an alternating kin group. The fact that Duncan was related to Malcolm II through a female line, rather than a male one, also gives us a reasonable indication that there was a lack of traditional candidates for the throne during this period.

It had only been a year since Gruoch's nephew Boite, last claimant to the throne through the male line, had been murdered. But there were two other grandsons born by daughters of Malcolm II, Macbeth and Thorfinn. Others may have viewed them as equally suitable or competent, if not more so, than Duncan. In practical terms, what the endorsement of Duncan by his grandfather really meant was that it would have left Duncan with a serious problem.

Kings of Alba were first and foremost war leaders. They had to protect their lands and to rule they needed respect from the noble class. Whatever Duncan's personal qualities were, as king, if they did not match up to the requirements of the age then there was a real possibility of challenges being raised. This was particularly so given that the tradition of alternating succession had been broken. As Macbeth looked longingly to the south, the wellbeing of Alba now depended on Duncan's actions.

The First Move

Winter would probably have passed quickly that year for Macbeth. Settled in one of his residences he might have spent his time hunting for the rich wildlife found in the woods; wild cattle, pigs, wolves and even bear. Meanwhile the bulk of the common population of Moray would have spent their time engaged in the production of craft goods. Gauging their days by the major festivals, only when the New Year had begun and the frosts began to disappear would they have returned to focus on the activities required for the new agricultural season.

Macbeth himself would have returned to the administration of Moray. This would include assessing what food rents to ask for in the coming months and planning how to keep his war band busy and loyal. But, in this particular year, 1035, Macbeth would have had a recurring thought in his head; what would Duncan do?

As part of the job, it was inevitable that the new King of Alba would try and prove his worth somewhere. Where, though, that was the question? We can guess that it didn't take too long for the answer to reach Macbeth from informants in the south. Presumably relishing his new-found power, Duncan's first target was his and Macbeth's cousin, Thorfinn Sigurdsson, the Raven Feeder[17].

Caithness and Orkney

As we found earlier, Thorfinn's father was the mighty Viking Sigurd, Earl of Orkney, and his mother was a Scottish daughter of Malcolm II. After his father was killed at the battle of Clontarf in 1014 Thorfinn was fostered out to his grandfather. We also speculated that it was highly likely that Thorfinn, Macbeth and Duncan all knew each other as boys. When Thorfinn grew older Malcolm II gave him the mainland Mormaership of Caithness, but the young ruler had to fight for his own Orkney inheritance.

In the early 11th century the Earls of Orkney were long-time settlers of the numerous islands that straddled the sea route between Scandinavia and the major trading centre of Dublin. Orkney was a major staging post on a route that drew many men into fortune-making and often troublesome schemes. The islands were also rich in agriculture and ruled by Thorfinn's half brothers.

It is likely that the relationship between Thorfinn and his brothers would have been as ambiguous as his relationship with Macbeth. At times rivals, at others allies, just as expected in the 11th century. What we identify from a number of texts[18] was that Thorfinn had a very independent nature. After a time he even travelled to meet the King of Norway to press his claim for a share of the Orkney Earldom. Meanwhile, back on Scottish soil, for a number of years he had refused to pay tribute to Alba for the Overlordship of Caithness.

It was here, in Caithness, at the northernmost tip of the Scottish mainland that Duncan decided to attack Thorfinn. Duncan despatched a commander named Muddan northwards with an army. He set up camp in Thurso but he was surprised by a sudden Viking attack. Muddan was defeated and fled. This now meant that Duncan himself had to enter the fight with Thorfinn.

King on the Water

Duncan sped north with eleven warships towards Orkney.[19] Sea travel was well known to the Scots. Water borne transport was the quickest and most efficient way to carry men and goods. Manning large plank-built warships similar to Viking boats, and using oars and sail, the Alba crewmen would have consisted primarily of commoners.

Obligated to give service to their king when he called, a percentage of men from differing areas would have been chosen to travel north with Duncan. Those left behind would have ensured that the crops were looked after. Onboard, there would have been professional seamen with the raiding party, such as boat captains, and there could have been as many as 50 men on each ship. However, in this sort of enterprise the bulk of the crew would have served as both sailors and soldiers.

Whether Macbeth was asked for help by Duncan we will never know. It does seem unlikely though, given that the new King of Alba was flexing his muscles. He was out to teach a lesson, perhaps a subtle one to Macbeth as well as a bloody one to Thorfinn. If the three boys had been friends in their youth they were friends no longer. As Macbeth isn't directly mentioned in any records of this event it's a safe assumption that, once they'd sailed around the north eastern tip of modern day Buchan, Duncan and his boats probably headed straight for Orkney across the Moray Firth. This was instead of hugging the Moray coast and perhaps landing at Burghead, the famous promontory fort, for supplies.

Just picture the scene when Macbeth found out about the naval expedition. To envisage 11 boats striking directly at Viking Orkney, so soon after a land defeat, must have caused astonishment. Macbeth might have considered that Duncan was either underestimating the opposition, or overestimating himself. But Duncan's ships surprised Thorfinn off Deerness and fierce fighting commenced. After a while Thorfinn managed to board Duncan's flagship, which prompted the King to jump overboard and scramble onto another ship. Perhaps not unexpectedly, the outcome for Duncan was another defeat. This included the loss of his flagship with a soaking for himself and the crew.

The Battle of Torfness

Undeterred, the annals and sagas[20] tell us that Duncan then raised another army from the east to the west of Scotland. He also enlisted Irish mercenaries. This army moved to do battle with Thorfinn and the Viking host. They clashed at Tarbat Ness in Ross-shire. The saga histories[21] tell that here, *where the swords sang south of the Oykel river*, Thorfinn fought with *Karl Hundasson*. There is, again, no mention of Macbeth in this fight with Thorfinn. Even so, some historians believe that it was Macbeth rather than Duncan who led the Alban army[22].

This is unlikely for a number of reasons. For one, at this particular time it is improbable that a Mormaer of Moray could have raised an army outwith his region. For another, it is said that the attacker travelled northwards from Berwick, deep within Lothian, a region gained for Alba by Malcolm II in 1018. This far south was the realm of Duncan. Assuming also that the Irish mercenary contingent probably came from the south west, where Duncan had previously ruled, then it is most probable that Macbeth, and Moray, played no part in the battle of Torfness.

With Moray sitting waiting on an outcome, Duncan's army could either have made its way north by a western route, or possibly travelled again by boat across the Moray Firth. On the day of the battle Macbeth might even have watched the proceedings from the top of the impressive Pictish fort at Burghead (C2), an ancient seat of power. In the distance, close to where he had stood in 1020, Macbeth would have seen Duncan's superior forces being overcome. Duncan then fled and what followed, according to Viking sagas, was that Thorfinn mustered a large force and invaded Alba.

Much more realistic is that the Vikings chased Duncan back south before he reached safety in his Tayside powerbase. By raiding any unlucky communities on the way down and back, the Vikings demonstrated that they had successfully protected their own interests. If this were the case, then it is certain that the unhappy folk memories of the villages savaged by Thorfinn would have added to the overall perception that Duncan's military reputation had taken a very big fall.

Macbeth's motives in not joining in may have been self preservation, but given his probable strong character, this seems unlikely. More on the cards, Macbeth was playing a strategic game, biding his time. At the year end, in November 1035, the mighty Canute, ruler of England and Scandinavia died. The world was changing and this would have given Macbeth further cause to think on what to do.

The Pot Simmers

As 1036 began we have no way of knowing whether Macbeth had formulated ambitious plans or not. Indeed, very little is known of the following four years of Duncan's reign. We can only assume that this was a fallow period in the high drama of Alba. Anyone waiting for Duncan to try and prove his prowess again would have to wait a little longer, including Macbeth and Thorfinn.

During the summer seasons Thorfinn probably raided up and down the west coast. We have no evidence of what Macbeth did during this period. He may have remained close to Moray, possibly only raiding adjacent lands to keep his war band active. In Moray itself though, he would have moved about from royal residence to royal residence. These are perhaps best described as domestic fortified places that also served as the centre of localised agricultural units. Here, collections of tribute were stored in safe places ahead of distribution or consumption.

Sometimes sited on hills, these residences were probably surrounded by ramparts and ditches, partly for defence and also to keep animals out. In Moray we believe they might have run in a chain from Inverness in the west, through Auldearn, Brodie, Forres,

Burghead and Elgin to Mortlach on the eastern border. There are so many ancient hill forts in Scotland that it is very difficult to distinguish between those from early medieval times and earlier ones unless dateable remains are found. To this day the exact location of Macbeth's Moray residences remain a mystery.

Further south, in 1038, the chess pieces began to move again. In this year Earl Eadulf came to power in Northumbria and ravaged Cumbria. We do not know precisely whether this meant modern Cumbria, or whether Eadulf ventured as far north as Strathclyde, but, as was the way, it was probably to prove his martial skill and build prestige. We also know that Duncan was still an overlord of territories in the areas, as was his brother Maldred who was married to Eadulf's sister. What the relationship between the half brothers was is open to speculation. In the end Duncan did not retaliate, not immediately that is.

Durham

Rather, Duncan waited patiently until early 1040 before raising an army to march into the heart of Northumbria. Here he laid siege to the great Christian settlement of Durham. Why he did this has been debated ever since. Durham was not an easy target. It was an emerging town, rich and prosperous, with a monastery set high above the River Wear. This made Durham very defendable, something the generation after Malcolm II, who had been repulsed and defeated at this location in 1006, would have remembered.

The events in Cumbria back in 1038 had not even threatened the Lothian lands in the east, obtained by Alba in 1018, so perhaps Duncan had planned a full blown invasion. If this was the case then it was most probably planned the year before. Interestingly, Harold Harefoot, the King of England, died in March 1040. This occurred by chance just as Harold's half brother, Harthacanute, was preparing an invasion of England with his Danish army. It might just have been, after all, a good time to try and seize Northumbrian territory and consolidate Alba's geographical borders. Success here would restore Duncan's reputation.

Given that Duncan's march on Durham was much more than a raiding party he would have had to call on traditional obligations to man his army. This would have required a considerable number of men and higher levies of individuals would have been taken away from the land when compared to the Orkney episode. An expedition such as Durham would not have been taken lightly given the potential for heavy losses. This was more so considering the historic tension between the northern and southern parts of Alba. Assuming Macbeth and Moray again played no part, it is probable that Duncan raised his men only in Angus, Fife and Lothian, with probable help from the south west of Scotland.

The invading force would have comprised men from all sections of the social hierarchy. A major muster point would have been set up and before the army marched south it would have drank heartily to victory. Word of its advance would have spread before it, and the Northumbrian leaders would have signalled for their own muster point, possibly Durham. Duncan probably came to Northumbria expecting open combat rather than a siege. Significantly, the result was disastrous. Duncan lost heavily and, as he raced back into Alba, the heads of his defeated warriors were hoisted up on spears around Durham.

Rebellion

In Alba, now was the time for any nobles pressing for change to make their move. We can imagine powerful voices, maybe led by the northern based Mormaers, speaking out against King Duncan. His crime was twofold; he had not taken the kingship, it had been given to him, and he had now suffered major defeats on two fronts. As a war leader Duncan was simply not up to the mark.

In Moray it is highly likely that Macbeth realised now was the time to make a move if he was ever to gain the kingship for himself. And why not? Duncan, descended through a female line, was not exactly bringing prestige to the kingdom. Macbeth not only had a similar claim to Duncan's, through his grandfather, but Macbeth also held the claim of his stepson Lulach, descended from Kenneth III.

Macbeth's standing in the court of Alba and his strong rule in Moray would have been noted by the other nobles. We make an assumption here that Macbeth was well connected. This would require strategic acumen and good communication skills. Whether or not an actual rebellion began in Alba, it is likely that discontent spread quickly. A strong character was now required and Macbeth fitted the bill. Interestingly, not too many years after Macbeth made his intent public, another strong character called Harold Godwinson seized power in England. But before this, Macbeth was about to face his own test.

Duncan made the next move. He had to regain prestige after the defeat at Durham and what better way than to quell unrest at home. Assuming that he had suffered heavy losses at Durham, he would have found it difficult to press a large force together. This, combined with the fact that speed was probably essential, makes it likely that Duncan travelled north by sea along the east coast. He might not have been able to muster more than four or five boat-loads, numbering perhaps 250 men in total. This group would try and nip any potential rebellion in the bud.

Preparation in Moray

Anticipating Duncan's possible moves, Macbeth would surely have added warriors to his existing war band and begun to prepare for a decisive encounter. The key members of his seasoned war band would have been mounted, using small local horses. The rest, including any called-up farmers, would have served as foot soldiers.

In terms of weapons the seasoned host would have used swords for single handed fighting, with scabbards of wood or leather. Round or rectangular shields were commonly used, with central bosses for deflecting weapon strokes and back straps for holding on tightly. The bulk of the force would probably have used spears, either light javelin types for throwing or larger and longer ones for thrusting. We assume here that the lighter types may have been more common in the circumstance, where speed of travel was of the essence.

Regarding other equipment, axes, often favoured by Vikings, may also have been used, as might slingshots and stones. We believe that elite warriors in Anglo Saxon war bands wore chainmail shirts, but we don't know whether Macbeth and his kin had use of these. However, they would have worn battle shirts of some design, possibly made of leather. Similarly helmets may have been worn by Macbeth and his immediate generals, but again this cannot be confirmed.

Evidence of metal working has been present in the Inverness area since very early times. Perhaps whilst overseeing new weapons being forged Macbeth decided on his plan. He would have been well acquainted with the key entry routes into Moray used by invading forces; either by sea, through the Great Glen or across the passes over the Mounth, the upland barrier separating Moray from Alba. Not knowing which one Duncan would use it made sense for Macbeth to gather his force at a central location affording rapid deployment. His presumed fort at Forres, on top of Cluny Hill, was perfect.

One Day in 1040

Once Macbeth's lookouts posted news of Duncan's approach, further east, by boat, Macbeth probably gathered his men at the base of the hill. Here, the impressive Sueno's Stone (c3), with its carvings depicting historic victories, was a worthy place to rouse men's emotions and build their spirits. Macbeth would have spoken clearly about what was at stake. This was nothing less than death or the kingship. Try to imagine the scene, shrieking warriors, some possibly tattooed, stirring themselves for battle. Perhaps Gruoch looked down from the wooden fort. If she did so as the men of Moray began to march east to counteract Duncan's supposed landfall, she must have realised there was a strong chance that she was looking at Macbeth for the last time.

In 1040 the geography of Moray was very different to what it is today. The sea swept right into what is now farmland through Loch Spynie, at that time a long extended arm of the sea that breached the modern coastline to the east of Lossiemouth. It then reached as far as the line of the modern B9012, perhaps even up to the B9013, before it petered out in salt marshes. Almost 1,000 years earlier, in Roman times, Burghead and Lossiemouth had probably formed an island totally separated from the mainland. In practical terms what this meant was that the route Macbeth's war band took, if they left from Forres, paralleled the modern A96 road to Elgin, with open seawater on their left for most of the way.

As Macbeth's force approached the area where the Bishop's Palace now stands at Pitgaveny (C4) they would have spied Duncan's beached ships. In the 11th century this area served as a port for the hinterland of Elgin. It would have been easier for Duncan to land here and offer battle than further east or west. To the east his men would have had to cross the river Spey and to the west he would have come up against the sea-fort at Burghead and its major defences.

Once Duncan landed at Pitgaveny we assume that he camped his force over the brow of the hill, where Pitgaveny Estate now stands. There he prepared once again for battle. His opponent was now Macbeth, who would have taken about four hours to reach him. When Duncan's lookouts sighted Macbeth's war band the alarms would have been sounded.

A Decisive Encounter

Approaching along the old shoreline from the west Macbeth and his men would have gathered one final time. This was when an 11th-century leader had to lead from the front. After Macbeth's final exhortations any fear would have been downplayed, as befits a warrior society, and banners and flags unfurled, battle horns sounding out. It is difficult for people today to appreciate what it was like to build up a fighting frenzy. But, standing near the spot where the advance could have begun, you can imagine the fear when just over the hill was possible death.

Macbeth's attacking force may have used their horses to charge at speed over the hill in order to try and destabilise Duncan in his temporary camp. This ploy often literally frightened the enemy into fleeing before real hand-to-hand fighting actually commenced. Following on quickly behind would have been the foot-soldiers, joining the warriors on horses who would have dismounted after the charge.

Trying to communicate in a melee, which could have involved up to five hundred men, would have been very difficult. Macbeth and Duncan would both have been in the thick of the fight. Their men would have regularly tried to see where they were as 11th century warlords often died in battle. This in itself could be the decisive battle event and so it was at Pitgaveny. The annals[23] tell of Macbeth himself delivering a fatal blow to Duncan, striking a mortal wound.

Following a Wounded King

It is said that on being wounded Duncan was carried from the field[24] by his retainers, who probably headed towards the 11th century hamlet of Elgin. Looking at the geography of the area this is highly probable. Macbeth would have seen the manoeuvre and made to follow the wounded king in order to finish him off. After crossing the river Lossie, Duncan presumably could travel no longer and was probably laid down to rest on a grassy knoll just to the east of the settlement. On this spot the ruin of a later 12th century cathedral now stands (C5).

We can speculate that as Mormaer, Macbeth headed straight for Elgin itself. From there he could have stood and watched as Duncan's retinue crowded around their dying leader. Soon, Duncan died[25] and Macbeth's path to the kingship of Alba was open. This major skirmish at Pitgaveny can be viewed therefore as a short but definitive civil war.

Duncan's men, if they were politically astute, did not have to contemplate death, flight, or even enslavement. Having travelled north to quell a powerful subject, who had then defeated them and who now needed support from all parts of Alba, it is highly likely that they made immediate overtures of peace to Macbeth.

Duncan's reign had not brought success to Alba. Rather, it had hardened internal wounds. A powerful new ruler was required to mend the situation. Macbeth was of royal descent, he was entitled to press a claim, and he was the stepfather of Lulach with an alternative claim to the throne. However, first and foremost, with the possible exception of Earl Thorfinn in the north, Macbeth was probably the most vigorous and martial leader available to Alba. But that was the future, first there was the aftermath of the battle to handle.

The costs of warfare were great. Friends and companions would have been killed and they would never grace the drinking halls again. Whilst preparing to celebrate victory Macbeth would also have mourned his losses but there was now little doubt that he would soon take the kingship of Alba.

Messengers would have been despatched to Gruoch informing her of her husband's victory and bidding her to prepare for a journey to Scone. Macbeth needed to seal the goodwill of the lords of Alba and be formally and properly inaugurated as the new king[26]. Macbeth, the 'Red King'[27] would rule in Alba, and there was much to do.

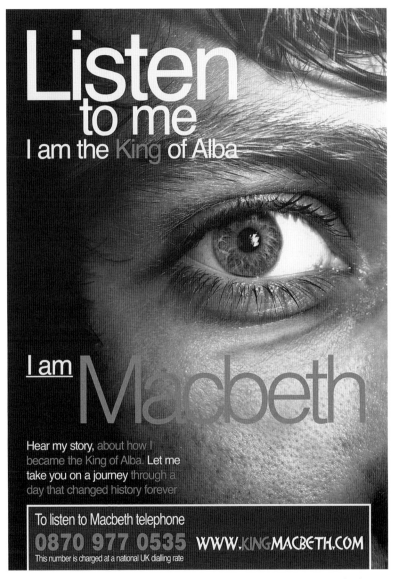

Poster promoting the King Macbeth audio story and web site www.kingmacbeth.com in the UK in conjunction with this book

© Seabridge Consultants

King of Alba

The Lady Gruoch heard the approaching horsemen and composed herself. Waiting at Forres for most of the day, the ritual of the prayers led by the monks new-arrived from Birnie had provided some comfort. Still, her mind raced. Had Macbeth succeeded or failed? Everything depended on it.

The message was a simple one, breathlessly delivered. Duncan dead; Macbeth unhurt and already on his way southwards towards Scone in a ship seized from Duncan's war band. 'Lulach, my son' said Gruoch to the boy by her side, 'we appear to have acquired a Kingdom'.

CHAPTER 4

King of Alba

Scone – the heart of the Kingdom

IT WAS ESSENTIAL for Macbeth to travel swiftly to Scone following the death of King Duncan. We assume that some at least of Duncan's nobles were with him at Pitgaveny where he was defeated and fatally wounded, and it is likely that Macbeth knew many if not all of the others well, but while Macbeth's claim to the throne was a good one – doubly so because of Gruoch's own royal lineage – he would have been only too aware of other potential claimants. Being inaugurated as King was a priority.

Scone, strategically located at the lowest point at which the River Tay could be forded, had been important since Pictish times and it is probable that the site was used for open air meetings and gatherings. Gathering places such as this were a focus for public life, law-making and the exercise of personal power and influence. In the Viking world such sites were known as 'tings'.

In the 9th or early 10th century Scone became the traditional inauguration place of the Kings of Alba and as a consequence the location took on an enormous strategic and symbolic significance. Here, in the sub-region of Gowrie, was the heart of the kingdom. The Moot Hill (D1), as it became known, was possibly an ancient barrow or chambered cairn and its raised height made the inauguration of a King a very visible, public act. The Stone of Destiny, today once again back in Scotland[28] after its removal by Edward I of England in 1297 and long years of exile at Westminster Abbey in London, stood on the hill and Kings must have sat on it or more likely stood on it during the rituals that marked a royal claimant's succession to the kingship. Given their claim to Irish ancestry, the Kings of Alba very probably modelled the inauguration ceremonies on Irish ones, blending pagan and Christian beliefs in ways that linked land and people and people and King. The 11th century Prophecy of Berchan refers to Scone as 'of the high shields' and 'of melodious shields'[29] so we can imagine that the inauguration of a new King was as much an acclamation by those present as it was a religious ceremony.

This blending of pagan and Christian beliefs is not as strange as it might seem. Christianity was still a relatively new religion and would have sat side by side with more ancient beliefs. The Celtic Christianity of the period was perhaps more tolerant than High Medieval Roman Christianity was to become. It is likely that there was a Celtic monastic community and church at or near the Moot Hill, providing an intellectual, administrative and of course religious resource for Kings of Alba. The Church would have been keen to position itself as a crucial part of the inauguration process, drawing authority from its role while at the same time symbolising its authority through the very exercise of it. The first recorded event at Scone is in 906 in an entry in the *Chronicle of the Kings of Alba*:

> ... and in his sixth year King Constantine and Bishop Cellach vowed together with the Gaels, to maintain the laws and disciplines of the faith and the rights of churches and of gospel-books on the Hill of Faith close to the royal civitas of Scone.[30]

The link between kingship and faith and the apparent dependency of one on the other is very evident.

In order to be inaugurated as King, Macbeth had to have the support of the church. He may have sought support in advance of his defiance of Duncan or more likely he entered into some hard bargaining when he arrived at Scone. The same bargaining would have gone on with the other Mormaers. Not all would have accompanied Duncan on his incursion into Moray and Macbeth had to win support in advance of the inauguration ceremony.

He was clearly successful in establishing his right to the kingship and so on Scone's Moot Hill, surrounded by his supporters, the nobility of Alba and church leaders, he was inaugurated as King of Alba. Thus began what we might describe as the *Macbethean* period in Alba's history.

The Nature of Kingship

So what was the nature of the kingship Macbeth enjoyed? We have seen that the young Macbeth was fostered at the royal court so he would have been familiar with the role of a king. In any case his time as Mormaer in Moray – arguably acting as a sub-king – was not so different from being ruler of the whole of Alba and we can assume that he remained as Mormaer even after he became King.

The world of Macbeth was a profoundly Celtic one, a culture and society that united Ireland and Alba. This Gaelic culture celebrated its heroes – kings were war leaders whose prestige depended on their prowess and success – while at the same time requiring its heroes to look after the interests of the extended families that made up the tribe. Kingship was not the 'divine right' that it was to become centuries later and the highly structured, hierarchical feudal world of the High Middle Ages had not evolved.

We have mentioned that kingship was not hereditary and that, in the Gaelic culture of the time, the royal succession alternated between collateral lines. The designated king-in-waiting was drawn from a pool of candidates, ensuring that only the most vigorous became King. It was King Malcolm II's decision to undermine this principle by designating Duncan as his successor that caused the resentment that led, ultimately, to the death of Duncan at Macbeth's hand.

When Macbeth became King of Alba he would have continued to travel around, accompanied by his followers, churchmen and administrators, staying at various locations around his kingdom in the same way as he had as Mormaer. Royal and Mormaer lands were managed by so-called thanes, the most basic rank of nobility, relieving itinerant lords and kings of the burden of day-to-day local administration. But there would still have been much to do alongside more enjoyable pursuits such as hunting and feasting.

Politics in the 11th century was all about the application of power, often in the form of military might exercised by the leader and his followers. The few documentary records of Macbeth's kingship that survive tell us nothing about how he consolidated power on becoming King, but it is probable that he did as kings had done before and sought out a military adventure in order to demonstrate his prowess and test the allegiance of his new subjects. The chronicles make no mention of where Macbeth decided to test himself and his men so perhaps it was neither a triumph nor a disaster. Unlike his two predecessors, Malcolm II and Duncan I, Macbeth's early prestige did not suffer at the gates of Durham.

Not everything was settled by violent means, of course. Marriage alliances were important in preventing warfare. Macbeth's own marriage to Gruoch was probably a political act though we might imagine that their relationship was much more than simply a duty. Undoubtedly, as King and Queen, Macbeth and Gruoch will have discussed the need to arrange other political matches. Perhaps, also, they reflected on their own situation, especially if what for them began as a political match quickly became a love match.

In ruling Alba Macbeth must have had advisers, perhaps churchmen – the intellectual elite of the time. Those same advisers, and others, would have been needed to advise him regarding foreign affairs, for Alba was part of a wider world. We will look at this world in the next chapter, but for now it is tempting to imagine Macbeth, the new King of Alba, remembering his meeting with King Canute and pondering the possibilities of winning such power and prestige for himself and Alba.

Abbot Crinan and Dunkeld

If Scone can be described as the heart of Alba then perhaps Dunkeld can claim to be the head, for the presence of Celtic Christian monks made it an important centre of learning. There was a Christian settlement there as early as the 6th century but the area really came to prominence in 849 when relics of St Columba were brought from

Iona, presumably to keep them safe from Viking raids. Dunkeld then became the headquarters of the Church in Alba though this status was lost to St Andrews in the 10th century when St Columba's relics were moved there. Dunkeld's location made it a place of strategic importance even in Pictish times, with the hills providing commanding positions for fortifications and good fertile farmland nearby.

The magnificent cathedral ruins (D2) in Dunkeld today date from long after Macbeth and Crinan's time, possibly overlying earlier less substantial Celtic buildings. Despite this, modern visitors to the town still get a strong sense of the ancient history and power of the place. Its fortunes may have waxed and waned but it remained throughout a special place.

Macbeth would have known Dunkeld from his time at the court of King Malcolm but it is unlikely that he was made especially welcome there in 1040 when he became King. The late King Duncan's father was Abbot Crinan, lay Abbot of the monastery and Diocese of Dunkeld. He may also have been Mormaer of Atholl but whether this is the case or not he was a powerful and wealthy person. It is said that he was born around 980 in Dunfermline, Fife, son of an early Lord of the Isles. His marriage to King Malcolm II's daughter Bethoc around 1000 points to him being very much part of the ruling elite: there must have been compelling political reasons for the match.

Since there are no records of who attended Macbeth's inauguration as King we do not know whether Crinan was present at Scone to see his son's killer claim the Kingship in his place. Given the proximity of Dunkeld to Scone he may have had no choice but to be there. We can well imagine him burning with hatred and vowing privately to see his grandsons avenged in due time, while swearing fealty to Macbeth for the present. To oppose him openly from the outset would have been foolish.

It would be surprising if the new King, Macbeth, spent much time in Dunkeld in the company of Crinan so the Abbot and his grieving wife would have been free to nurture their discontent and bide their time until opportunity arose or patience wore out. Probably their first priority was the safety of their grandchildren, Duncan's two sons Donald Ban and Malcolm. Later histories suggest that the boys – Donald Ban aged six or seven but Malcolm perhaps a few years older – remained in Alba for two years, during which time Macbeth tried to find and eliminate them, but there is no contemporary evidence to corroborate this[31].

It seems thereafter that Donald Ban was sent to the Western Isles for safety while the eldest brother, Malcolm, went to the household of Earl Siward of Northumbria. Siward was a distant relative of Malcolm's and, as a close neighbour and political rival of Alba, would have had more than enough reason to want to harbour a claimant to the Alban throne. Malcolm appears to have gone on to be a protégé of King Edward (the Confessor) of England, who granted him lands in Northamptonshire.

An alternative scenario sees Malcolm taking refuge in the north rather than the south, where he was taken in by Earl Thorfinn in Orkney. From this power base, some would argue, Malcolm was later to launch his invasion of Alba[32]. But that is for a later chapter in our story. Our view here is that whether or not Malcolm spent time with Thorfinn in Orkney there is evidence of a strong connection between Malcolm and the English court and a keen – and active – Northumbrian interest in Alban affairs.

This Northumbrian connection to Malcolm and the so-called (though not at the time) 'House of Dunkeld' had deep roots. Duncan I, whom Macbeth had removed so decisively from the throne of Alba, had a half brother called Maldred. Maldred was married to Ealdgyth, daughter of Earl Uhtred of Northumbria and therefore grand-daughter of King Ethelred (the Unready) of England. This is the same Earl Uhtred who we met in Chapter 3 where he was defeated by Malcolm II at the Battle of Carham in 1018 and subsequently assassinated by King Canute as punishment for his failure and the loss of Lothian north of the Tweed to Alba. Now Earl Siward of Northumbria, himself also related to the House of Dunkeld, saw an opportunity to restore some Northumbrian prestige at the expense of Macbeth.

First Crisis for Macbeth

In 1045, perhaps as part of a concerted plan to defeat Macbeth and put Maldred on the throne of Alba (Duncan's sons being too young), the apparent or relative peace of Alba was broken and Macbeth faced his first real crisis. The *Irish Annals* record that:

> A battle was fought between Scots, upon a united expedition; and Crinan, Abbot of Dunkeld, was killed in it, and many along with him, namely nine score fighting men.[33]

We might interpret this as a coup attempt by Crinan while the Alban host was gathered perhaps, given the events to follow in 1046, in preparation for an anticipated invasion from Northumbria. The number of dead – 180 – suggests that this was no mere skirmish and we can conjecture that the need for personal leadership in battle meant that Crinan probably met his death at the hand of King Macbeth. We do not know where this took place though logic might suggest that it was in the south of Alba.

First Duncan and now Crinan, his father. If the exiled young Malcolm harboured thoughts of revenge for the death of his father he was to be disappointed on this occasion. Instead he had to mourn the death of his grandfather. There is some debate about how the crisis continued. The *Annals of Durham* record that in 1046:

> Earl Siward came to Scotland with a great army and expelled King Macbeth and appointed another, but after his departure Macbeth recovered the kingdom.[34]

Interpretation of this entry in the *Annal* has proven difficult. If the date of 1046 is correct it suggests that Earl Siward was either belatedly trying to support Crinan's 1045 coup attempt, or he was simply keeping the pressure up on Macbeth as part of a long term plan of action, possibly initiated in concert with the unsuccessful Crinan.

If the date of 1046 is incorrect it could be argued that the events recorded under the year 1046 occurred in 1045 or even 1054. The former would suggest that Siward was acting in direct concert with Crinan, trying to catch Macbeth in a pincer movement from both inside Alba and out-with the kingdom. The latter would tie in with a later, better corroborated crisis for Macbeth. Our view is that the date was 1045 or 1046 and, whichever of those is correct, Siward was acting in support of Abbot Crinan's faction.

The other point of interpretation of the entry in the Annals of Durham is the statement that Macbeth was expelled and another was appointed in his place. We tend to agree with those who regard the most likely explanation to be a temporary reverse for Macbeth in the south of Alba, perhaps the Lothians. The 'other' who was appointed does not appear to have been Duncan's son Malcolm but an intriguing and not so unlikely alternative is that it was Duncan's half brother Maldred. We saw earlier that he had a close connection with Northumbria and placing him in control of a recaptured Lothians may have been a logical thing for Earl Siward to do.

The Annals do not help us with this identification, however, and in any case Macbeth took advantage of Earl Siward's departure to recapture the territory he had lost. Maldred, if it was indeed him, was forced out. We do not know whether Maldred had a serious ambition to become King of Alba. Perhaps he was just another political pawn in the endless game of Alban power politics. He seems, in any case, to have turned his dynastic ambitions elsewhere because his son Gospatric was to become Earl of Northumbria under William the Conquerer.

With his first crisis weathered, Macbeth could concentrate on developing his relationships with Alban society, fostering the stability that gave Alba the productive seasons noted by the chroniclers and creating the security that was ultimately to enable Macbeth to leave the Kingdom on pilgrimage. What, then, was the nature of Alban society?

Alba: a Celtic Society

Scotland can be regarded as comprising five different 'ancestral' peoples distinguished by their cultures and languages. The Picts and the Britons were indigenous, to be joined over time by Vikings from the north and west, Angles from the south and Scots, a Celtic people, from Ireland.

By the beginning of the 11th century it was the Scots with their Gaelic culture and language who were in the ascendancy. Some have described Macbeth as the last of the Celtic Kings of Alba. After his death and that of his stepson and successor Lulach, Alba – or Scotland as it was to become – the Celtic world was in retreat and the structures society were changing, reflecting the wider changes afoot across the continent of Europe.

We need to be very careful not to apply our current notions of society and how it operates to that of 11th century Alba. We need to be careful, also, because Alban society was not a single homogenous thing; it had regional variations reflecting the different histories of the provinces that made up the kingdom. Nevertheless we can describe Alban society in general terms.

The two principal pillars of society were land and kindred. Wealth depended ultimately on land so the success of the agricultural economy was an essential prerequisite for the maintenance of society. Kindred – that connected group we might otherwise call clan or tribe – was of paramount importance and an individual's responsibility was to act in the best interests of the kindred. This is a very different situation to today where we tend to operate on an individual basis and family ties are of less importance, but Celtic society had different values to those which we take as read today.

At the top of society was the King, the first among a group of otherwise near equals, each ruling a Province of Alba. These men – and society appears to have been male dominated, at least from what we can tell from the little evidence that remains to us – were the real power within the kingdom. They were the *Mormaers*, the highest-ranking members of society outside the royal kindred.

This 'ranking' of society can be understood most easily

through legal documents setting out the compositional payments in respect of killings and woundings. In such documents the value of each rank of society is expressed not in monetary terms – Scottish coinage did not exist in our period – but as numbers of cattle or 'kine'

Woolf summarises payments due for a killing, or 'cro' as follows:[35]

1,000 kine	King	
150 kine	King's son	*comes* (ie mormaer)
100 kine	son of a *comes*	Thane
66.66 kine		Thane's son
44.44 kine		Thane's grandson *octigern*
16 kine		*rusticus*

While the accuracy of individual legal documents and their applicability to the whole of the kingdom can be challenged, and the interpretation of the various terms is sometimes difficult, what is clear is that there were different levels in society and Mormaers were near the top.

The origin of the term *Mormaer* is not known for certain and there are varying interpretations. It may be of Pictish origin and refer to the position of regional king or sub-king, or it may be a term for a position appointed by the king. Provincial Mormaers may have been drawn from particular Scots kindreds, such as the Cenel Loairn in Moray. We simply don't know for sure. Equivalent modern terms might be Great Steward, Duke or Count, but these words have more modern connotations that probably do not fully capture the nature of Mormaer-ship.

The Mormaer was the leading man in the province. He may not necessarily have been the biggest landowner but he was the most powerful and influential individual. In addition to managing his own lands he would have been responsible for enforcing the king's justice, and for leading the men of the province in war.

The next stratum of society was the thanes, locally powerful individuals generally acting as royal officials and managing land on their behalf. Mormaers may well have had men filling the same function though the name might be different: local leaders with the relative wealth and power to exercise authority, including the collection of rents. The network of thanes, each associated with a different 'shire' (a local area for which the thane was responsible and which formed the basis of later parish organisation), gave the king local influence and in-kind revenue opportunities. It also perhaps acted as something of a counterweight to the power of the Mormaers. There is no evidence that Mormaers were also thanes so we must see Shakespeare's attribution of the title of Thane of Cawdor to Macbeth as either a misunderstanding or a deliberate belittling of Macbeth's status. We are not even certain that the term *thane* was in widespread use in the early 11th century.

The middle managers of 11th century society were the freeholders, variously called 'hiredmen', 'drengs' or 'husbandmen'. These men were expected to pay tribute or rent in kind, and to serve in the common army if their lord required. They provided local community leadership and stability. Beneath them were a variety of generally un-free people with various degrees of economic independence all the way down to virtual slavery.

In general Celtic Alban society was not so very different from that of the rest of Britain, but more conservative, less open to change and closer to life in Ireland than life in England.

So in summary Macbeth's world was a Celtic one, in which ideas of kindred, family and household were fundamental and social mobility was slight. There was a social order based on relationships of mutual obligation between people rather on the top-down land-holding hierarchy of duties and obligations that was the basis of feudalism throughout much of later medieval Europe.

Existing alongside this social structure based on land and kindred stood the intellectual elite – the poets, musicians and priests of Alba. Leaders like Macbeth would have had household poets to entertain them and also to record significant events. This was an oral tradition with ancient roots. It may be the words of Macbeth's court poet we hear when he is described in the Prophecy of Berchan as *'The red, tall, golden-haired one, he will be pleasant to me among them; Scotland will be brimful west and east during the reign of the furious red one.*[36] It is likely, too, that they would have had court musicians, harpists and singers perhaps, whose role it was to entertain and divert the king, his household and guests.

The best educated people in the kingdom would have been churchmen, members of the distinctive Celtic Church engaged in God's work.

God's work

In the year 563 an Irish missionary was banished to Scotland. This monk was called Colum Cille and we know him today as St Columba, the founder of the monastery on Iona and the man who converted the Pictish King Bridei to Christianity. So began the Christianisation of all the peoples of Scotland and by Macbeth's time Alba was a Christian kingdom. It may well be that it was the shared Christian faith of the people of Alba that enabled the kingdom to gain in strength despite the diversity of their origins.

The lack of documentary evidence for the early church in Alba makes an understanding of it difficult to achieve in detail but the broad outline can be described. Celtic Christianity took the place of even earlier pagan beliefs, churches often occupying existing physical locations as a way of practically, as well as symbolically, replacing the one with the other. This was a vibrant time for the church though the Viking raids that began at the end of the 8th century undoubtedly affected its development.

One distinctive feature of the Celtic church was its monastic tradition. Many clerics were not celibate so they and their families formed part of the local community, even if the community was a monastic one. Concerns about the stagnation of the Celtic church and worsening standards of behaviour among monks, led in the 9th century to a reform movement that spread to Alba from Ireland. The movement's adherents were known as the Celi De or 'servants of God' and we know them as the Culdees. They advocated stricter observance of monastic celibacy and a more ascetic lifestyle than was common among monks and the reform movement proved popular, with Culdee communities in such important locations as Dunkeld, Scone and St Andrews.

There was also a Culdee community on St Serf's island (D3) in Loch Leven in south-eastern Perth and Kinross. Here the fragmentary records of Alban history reveal that Macbeth and Gruoch made two grants of lands to the monks, demonstrating their religious faith and perhaps rewarding the monastery for services rendered or support provided. The land grants are made, so the records state, *'from motives of piety and for the benefit of their prayers' in the names of 'Macbeth son of Findláech and Gruoch, daughter of Boite, King and Queen of Scots.'*[37]

Throughout Western Europe there was a long tradition of royal grants of lands to monasteries, cementing relationships between church and political elite and creating a subtle network of mutual obligations, responsibilities and expectations. Some historians have conjectured that the grants to the Culdees of Loch Leven were made because of a connection between Gruoch and the area. If her ancestral origins lay in Fife this may indeed have been the case but it is just as possible that Macbeth and Gruoch knew the monks because of the journeys of the itinerant court through other parts of the kingdom where Culdee communities prospered. It is not too fanciful to imagine Macbeth feeling a special sense of obligation to the Culdees if it was the Culdee monks in Scone who officiated when he became King of Alba. In any case, by endowing a Culdee community the king and his queen were showing their approval of the reformed Celtic church, perhaps an important point for them to make.

Some people have seen Macbeth's grant-giving as an attempt to assuage feelings of guilt he felt at the 'murder' of King Duncan, but it is more likely that Macbeth and Gruoch were simply following established practice by granting land to the church.

Celtic monasteries, whether or not they were Culdee communities, were religious centres, of course, but they were also places of learning. Literacy was promoted by the church, which had an important educational role. The turbulent history of the church means that little written material survives from this early period. The only illustrated manuscript to survive from early medieval Scotland is the so-called *Book of Deer*, probably made at the Columban monastery at Deer in Aberdeenshire. As well as its original illuminated manuscript the *Book of Deer* contains later marginal notes, made in Gaelic in the early 1100s. The book, one of Scotland's most important manuscripts, is now housed in Cambridge University Library[38].

Monasteries provided the focus for a whole range of other activities including metal-working, leather-working and stone-carving, for example. In this they were the industrial centres of their day. They held lands to sustain them and had strong relationships with the leading families in their region, providing an educated religious and administrative resource in a symbiotic relationship between political and religious leadership. Monasteries were in the care of abbots rather than bishops. These abbots could be and often were laymen rather than clergy, fulfilling a range of leadership functions on behalf of their community. Abbots were closely connected with the political elite of Alba – consider for example Abbot Crinan of Dunkeld, father of a king, adversary of another and grandfather of another. These were powerful people, whatever their duty of care for their community of monks engaged in more spiritual activities, and most would have been war leaders if necessary, as Crinan was.

There is some evidence that bishops and sees existed in Alba, at least in some places, but the hierarchical organisation of the Roman church had not come to prevail. Parishes may have existed by default, coinciding with the boundaries of thanages and with small churches or chapels at their centre. We can imagine a landscape dotted with small timber and turf built churches, chapels and shrines for the living and cemeteries for the dead. There was no imposed order to this, just a matching of Celtic Christian religion with agricultural settlement. Few buildings were constructed of stone so there is little archaeological evidence for us to find today. The principal religious monuments to survive from this time are the monumental stone sculptures that still stand in many places.

Celtic Christianity in 11th century Alba was on the periphery of Christian Europe. It has been described rather unkindly, though probably accurately, as:

Diverse, unorganised and in some important respects markedly different from the Church of most of Western Europe.[39]

It is unlikely that King Macbeth considered the Celtic church to be especially diverse, unorganised and different until in 1050 he embarked on a pilgrimage to Rome where he would have seen Alba from a completely different perspective. There among the emerging kingdoms and empires of Europe and beyond lay the kingdom of heaven.

The Kingdom of Heaven

Rome; the spiritual heart of the Christian church, a place described to Macbeth in compelling detail by King Canute back in 1031. At the time, Macbeth had been more in awe of Canute than he cared to recall and Canute's words had never left him. Now, at last, it was time for Macbeth to see Rome for himself, to make his peace with God and the gatekeepers of the kingdom of heaven. There was politics to consider too, for the world was changing and Alba with it.

Macbeth turned to glare at the monks in his retinue, their excited babble breaking the peace of his thoughts.

CHAPTER 5

The Kingdom of Heaven

BY GOING ON PILGRIMAGE, Macbeth was following a long tradition of Royal pilgrimages, even if he himself may have been influenced by Canute's personal example. There were several pilgrimage destinations, with Rome second only to Jerusalem in importance. There were several reasons for this, the first and most obvious being the association with both St Peter and St Paul at Rome and the presence of the relics of several saints. The second reason was that the Pope, as Bishop of Rome, claimed precedence over the four other Patriarchs of the Christian church. The cathedral of the Bishop of Rome was, and still is, the Basilica of St John Lateran and not St Peters as many people think today. The Basilica contains the Papal throne and ranks above all the other churches in the Roman Catholic Church today. The third reason was more practical and political; as ruler of the Papal States, the Pope was a force to be reckoned with even if the fortunes of the States were to wax and wane. Rome combined spiritual and secular power, a compelling combination for kings contemplating their own mortality and wanting to leave their mark on the world outside their own kingdoms.

The portrayal of Macbeth as a usurper and tyrant in later chronicles, as well as in Shakespeare's drama, is rather at odds with the fact that he went on pilgrimage to Rome and, in doing so, came into direct personal contact with the medieval European world. It is worth considering Macbeth's pilgrimage in detail, and reflecting on what was happening elsewhere in Europe in the 11th century.

Macbeth's pilgrimage

The only near contemporary source for Macbeth's pilgrimage is a monk called Marianus Scotus. He was an Irish monk who was expelled from a monastery in Moville, County Down, in 1056 and subsequently preached and studied in continental Europe before entering the monastery of St Martin at Mainz in 1069. There he completed a *Chronicle of World History* – an ambitious title for a wandering monk – in 1073.

His Chronicle is believed by historians to be a fairly reliable source and for 1050 it reports that *'The King of Scots, Macbeth, scattered silver like seed to the poor in Rome.'*[40] The only conceivable reason for Macbeth to have been in Rome was on pilgrimage. In order to make the journey in time for one of the most significant dates in the Christian calendar, Easter, Macbeth would have had to begin his long journey in 1049. It says much for the security of his rule in Alba that he was able to leave his kingdom for an extended period though we have no evidence for the arrangements he left behind. Did, for example, Lulach – perhaps with Gruoch as advisor – act on his behalf during his absence? We do not know the answer. Lulach's nickname, 'the foolish' or 'the simpleton' might suggest that a wise king would have been loathe to leave him in charge, but the nickname could just as easily refer to the circumstances of Lulach's death rather than reflect opinion of him more generally.

Whatever the nature of the arrangements, however, Macbeth was confident enough to embark on a journey of some 1,200 miles. He and his retinue would probably have sailed down the east coast of Alba and then continued southwards skirting the east coast of England – a dangerous part of the journey, no doubt, and one that would have seen the boatmen take great care to avoid any mishaps that might require beaching the ships. Crossing the Channel, Macbeth was entering uncharted territory for him personally but his retinue would have included an experienced guide and the pilgrimage route through France or the Low Countries, perhaps via Reims and then onwards via the Alpine passes and into northern Italy.

If, as we think, Macbeth left Alba in 1049 he is likely to have aimed to arrive in Reims in time for the consecration of Reims Cathedral in October 1049. Here, Macbeth would have had the opportunity to meet with the Holy Roman Emperor Henry III and Pope Leo IX, major figures in 11th century European politics and religious life and probably attend one of Leo's reforming Councils. A second Council was held by Leo IX in Mainz later in 1049 so Macbeth could have attended that if he did not arrive in Reims before October. His political instincts would doubtless have led him to seek to reach Reims in time.

Leo IX, a reforming Pope

Leo IX was in important figure in the history of the Medieval Church. Born in Alsace in 1002 (and therefore of Macbeth's generation of leaders) and with the support of the Emperor Henry III he was elected Pope in February 1049 and made his reforming intentions clear by using the opportunity of his first Easter synod or council to reaffirm the requirement for clerical celibacy. Further decrees were issued at Reims in October, including against simony (the use of money to buy religious office) thereby continuing the momentum of reform.

We saw in earlier chapters that monasteries were an essential part of the fabric of life in 11th century Alba and the same was true elsewhere. Leo IX was particularly influenced by the reformin leadership of the Abbey of Cluny. Cluny's adherence to the Benedictine[41] monastic rule saw it the acknowledged leader of western monasticism from the late 10th century.

Not content to try and exercise his authority by staying in Rome, Leo IX travelled extensively, rather in the way that other medieval rulers exercised their own authority in person. His success in imposing Papal authority by reforming the church and in enforcing canon, or religious, law, as well as in re-establishing the prestige of the Papacy from a low point – only a few years previously there had been three Popes (Benedict IX, Gregory VI and Sylvester III) all at the same time – effectively laid the basis for the Roman Church as it is today. It would be surprising indeed if Macbeth had not heard of such an active, up-and-coming man of a similar age to himself and we might imagine that he hurried to Reims to have the opportunity to meet him and his supporter, the Emperor himself.

International politics

International politics in the 11th century were not mediated by the sort of diplomatic services modern countries use to manage their affairs. Instead it was a more personal business, with leaders prepared to treat with each other as required. The international communication network that made relationships between countries manageable was, however, the Church. Churchmen across the Christian world had a shared set of values and were able to communicate with each other in a common language whatever their geographical origin. As centres of learning, monasteries produced and housed intelligent men, some of whom would have become part of Royal households.

The presence of a universal Christian Church, therefore, helped politics 'work' and underpinned the importance of the Church itself. The fortunes of the Papacy might wax and wane but the Church itself was constant and integral to things. On his journey to Rome we can be certain that Macbeth would have had monks travelling as part of his retinue and these would have acted as advisers and facilitators as well as tending to their spiritual duties. They would have mediated some of the political relationships between the men of what was becoming a very dynamic Western Europe.

The dynamic West

The early medieval period had seen Byzantium, the successor to the eastern Roman Empire become rich and powerful. In the west, by contrast, riches and power were scarce in the centuries following the collapse of the Western Roman Empire. These were turbulent times and by the 10th-century people must have felt assailed from every side. From the south the Islamic Saracens were extending their power with Spain a key frontier between Christians and Muslims. From the north the Vikings traded and raided their way into the affairs of every kingdom and province they encountered, including England, Ireland and Alba as we have seen already. One group settled in the Duchy of Normandy and they were to have an enormously significant impact on the development of Western Europe. From the east came the Magyar or Hungarian peoples pushing relentlessly westwards until their defeat at the Battle of Lechfeld in 955.

But the West survived and out of the chaos came a time of revived fortunes. The German Empire of the 11th century was a solid political structure though it gradually lost out to the Frankish world that seemed more dynamic, perhaps because of the struggles between the various provincial dynasties and the lack of the centralising force of a strong monarchy. The development of feudalism was rapid, underpinned by a revived economic situation once Western European kingdoms had weathered the onslaughts of the Vikings, Magyars and Saracens. Economic revival provided the resources required for the feudal hierarchy to function.

It was in this dynamic environment that Pope Leo IX sought to build the authority of the church while at the same time playing a part in secular politics as the ruler of the Papal States. These covered a swathe of territory across Italy and the Pope ruled them in the same fashion as any other monarch. It was as a secular leader rather than as Pope that Leo IX met his downfall. As we saw earlier a group of Vikings had settled in France in what became known as the Duchy of Normandy. There they developed a reputation as mercenaries and in that capacity they quickly expanded into the Mediterranean. Arriving in Italy as mercenaries some of them stayed and fought for control of territory. They had two major enemies to fight – the Byzantines, who held the south of Italy as part of the Byzantine Empire; and an anti-Norman consortium put together by Leo IX. Leo's army attempted to combine with a Byzantine force to face the Normans together but was forced instead to fight them alone. At the battle of Civitate in 1053 Leo's army was defeated and the Pope was captured by the Normans. He died the following year and the Normans won themselves a kingdom in Southern Italy and Sicily.

East to Byzantium and the world beyond

Macbeth will have heard stories of the power and wealth of Byzantium, the eastern Christian bulwark against the Muslim world beyond. Perhaps from Alba the Byzantine Empire seemed remote and distant but on his arrival in Rome Macbeth will have been only too aware of its existence. The Empire included the southern part of Italy within its boundaries, not far from Rome. It is even possible that Macbeth's first contact with the effectiveness of Norman soldiery was while he was in Rome; Norman mercenaries were present there as well as in Byzantine service. As we will discover in the next chapter of Macbeth's story he was to make use of Norman fighting prowess himself in the future.

Beyond the Byzantine Empire was, to the east and south, a Muslim world that spread the whole way across the southern shores of the Mediterranean and into Spain. This was a vast, turbulent area, ruled for a time by the Abbasid caliphate in Baghdad but facing an ultimately successful challenge from the Turkish Seljuk Empire founded by Tugrul Beg in 1037. In due time Byzantium was to fall to Islamic conquest but before then it was to be joined in its wars against the expansionist Islamic world by western Christendom when the First Crusade was advocated by Pope Urban II in 1095. All these events, though, occurred long after Macbeth's story.

Further north from Byzantium were Hungary and Kievan Russia, places of which Macbeth knew about as much as rulers there knew of Alba. These were Christian kingdoms, but of a different kind to the church Macbeth knew. There was trouble in the church and a great rift was about to occur.

Schism in the church

The estrangement of the eastern and western branches of Medieval Christianity had deep and complex roots and the full story is beyond our scope here but we can point to the earlier split of the Roman Empire into an eastern, Greek portion and a Western, Latin portion and the growing cultural differences between the two. With linguistic unity broken, cultural unity eroded and political changes had massive impacts. Whereas the Western Roman Empire had been overrun by Germanic tribes the Eastern Empire continued to thrive and even tried to re-conquer the west. Meanwhile the two churches developed their own approaches and rites and arguments over precedence loomed larger.

Pope Leo IX, in line with his determination to reassert Papal authority, claimed that as Bishop of Rome he took precedence over the other four Patriarchs in the Christian church[42]. The focus for what became a dispute between Western and Eastern Christianity that came to a head in 1054 was the right to jurisdiction over a church in Sicily and resulted in mutual excommunications (not lifted until 1965) and a schism between east and west that remains in place today. If Macbeth and Pope Leo met, as we think is highly likely, and if the two men found a liking for each other, which is possible, then perhaps they talked of Leo's dispute and the likelihood that the Christian Church was about to split in two. It is an intriguing possibility.

Thorfinn's pilgrimage

Our digression into wider affairs has been instructive because it provides a context wider than just Alba and its neighbours but it is time to return to matters closer to home. Macbeth may have had an unlikely companion when he went on his pilgrimage to Rome in the person of Thorfinn Sigurdsson, Earl of Orkney; now a rival but, possibly, Macbeth's former childhood friend. The Orkneyinga Saga says that Thorfinn went on pilgrimage but neither it nor any other contemporary records say that he and Macbeth travelled together or even at the same time.

There must surely have been an understanding reached between these two rivals, because how else would they trust in the security of their respective dominions, and we might imagine that here once again Christian monks were able to broker a deal between the two rulers that gave each the confidence to make a lengthy journey to Rome. Did they in fact travel together in an uneasy companionship? Possible but perhaps rather unlikely because each man would have had his own wider political agenda in mind and neither would want the other to be privy to all their secrets or even know who they were talking to.

Who knows, perhaps Macbeth's 'scattering silver like seed to the poor' was as much to out-do Thorfinn as it was to help the poor of the city of Rome.

Back to Alba

His spiritual aim achieved by visiting the last resting place of St Peter, his sins acknowledged if not all atoned for and his head full of new experiences and with a wider perspective on the world, Macbeth would have made his long and weary journey back to Alba. It was a matter of retracing steps. Lots of them, back to an Alba that must have felt almost like a different place by the time Macbeth and his retinue returned to loved ones and friends. There was time for the stories to be told of the wonders that had been seen, and for life to get back to some routine before events were once again to move, this time towards a conclusion.

Birnie Kirk, site of an early Celtic church dedicated to St Brendan the Navigator. Macbeth and Gruoch may have married here and, if they did, the Celtic Coronach bell still there today would have rung out in celebration.

© Cameron Taylor

Mortlach church in the town of Dufftown is one of the oldest places of Christian worship in Scotland, founded in 566 by St Moluag. The Celtic monastic community here would have been a centre of learning at the eastern edge of Macbeth's Moray.

© Cameron Taylor

The Battle of the Seven Sleepers in 1054 marked the beginning of the end for Macbeth. Many think the site of the battle is Dunsinane Hill and this view from the top of the hill shows the dramatic nature of the terrain from which Macbeth led his force to battle.

© Cameron Taylor

Shakespeare linked Macbeth with Cawdor Castle but there is no historical evidence for this. The castle with its gardens is nevertheless a delightful place to visit.

© iStock International Inc.

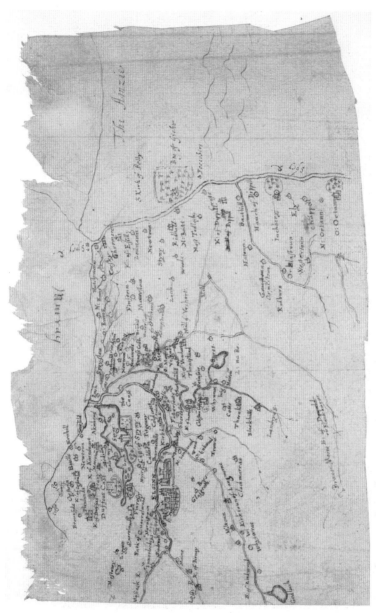

Extract from one of Timothy Pont's maps showing the area around Elgin in Moray. Note the loch of Spynie, now drained, and the place name 'Pitgeuny' i.e. Pitgaveny, where we believe Macbeth defeated and mortally wounded King Duncan. The map dates from the late 16th or early 17th century, at least 500 years after Macbeth's time.

The magnificent ruins of Elgin Cathedral, begun in the 13th century, stand where the wounded King Duncan was allegedly brought following his defeat at Pitgaveny. Duncan's death here cleared the way for Macbeth to become King of Alba in 1040.

Artist's impression by Peter Needham, showing three figures standing on Macbeth's Hillock near the village of Brodie in Moray.

© *Seabridge Consultants*

Spynie Palace was built as a residence for the Bishops of Moray long after Macbeth's time. The landscape here has changed dramatically with the draining of Spynie loch. The loch once gave direct access to the Moray Firth.

© Peter Needham

An artist's impression by Peter Needham, showing the scene at Pitgaveny as Macbeth arrives to confront King Duncan's invading force. The scene shows Spynie loch, now drained, just beside the modern car park at Spynie Palace.

© Seabridge Consultants

The island of Iona has a special place in Scotland's history. It was the earliest Christian settlement in Scotland and was the burial place of Scottish Kings and others of importance. The photograph shows the entrance to Iona Abbey, with a replica of the 8th century St John's Cross.

© iStock International Inc.

The earliest structures on Scone's Moot Hill have been replaced by later buildings, including this chapel. The original Stone of Destiny, removed from the Moot Hill by Edward I and kept in Westminster Abbey, London for centuries, is now back in Scotland in Edinburgh Castle.

© iStock International Inc.

Photograph of Sueno's Stone, a six metre high carved stone monument dating from before Macbeth's time. This impressive but enigmatic stone is now encased in a protective glass enclosure and is in the care of Historic Scotland.

© Cameron Taylor

Artist's impression by Peter Needham of Sueno's Stone showing a fortified residence on the hill overlooking the monument and a small settlement at what was to become Forres.

Cover for a musical score of Verdi's opera *Macbeth*, depicting Shakespeare's story of Macbeth and Banquo's encounter with the three witches on a blasted heath. While Macbeth was a real man, Banquo and the witches have no basis in fact.

© iStock International Inc.

The Wallace monument near Stirling and, in the foreground, a statue of Robert the Bruce. These celebrate the lives of two of Scotland's heroes. Surely there should also be a statue of an earlier hero, Macbeth?

© iStock International Inc.

The End of Many Things

IMAGINING THE PAST

The party weaved their way across the causeway guided by the King's riders. Macbeth himself stood watching from the hill. Taking in the sweep of Lothian he focused back on the group who had just travelled through his southern lands. They were already learning that to enter the heart of his kingdom was not that easy. A wry smile crossed Macbeth's ruddy face. Soon, his defences would be even better!

CHAPTER 6

The End of Many Things

THE GROUP CONSISTED of two Norman lords and their families and they probably reached Alba in early 1053. Macbeth may have met them near modern day Bridge of Allan. Here the Highland Boundary Fault has thrust up a line of hills that guard the approaches to the north. If our scenario actually occurred then it is conceivable that Macbeth could have stood above the modern ruins of Logie Church (E1). Founded for St Serf, this sits below a wooded crag to the west of Stirling University on the old drove road into the Ochil Hills. But what was Macbeth doing waiting for Normans to cross the salt marshes which, back then, made entering Alba seem almost like crossing over to an island?

Anglo Norman Relations

As ever, the crashing political waves that increasingly struck mainland Britain in the 11th century washed the southern shores of the island before hurtling in an arc northwards. In 1051 Godwin, the powerful Earl of Wessex, had been asked by King Edward the Confessor of England to harry, or besiege, his own population of Dover[43]. This was after the locals had fought with and killed Norman knights friendly to the King.

Godwin refused, and when Edward's troops moved to enforce the order, backed up by Earl Siward of Northumberland, Godwin fled across the English Channel to Bruges. This seemingly innocuous episode would eventually turn into the maelstrom that resulted in William the Conqueror defeating Godwin's son, Harold, at the Battle of Hastings in 1066. But that was the future.

Back in 1052, King Edward alienated his English Earls by appearing to favour the Norman incomers. As a result, the Earls changed allegiance and made overtures to Godwin. He returned to England with a vengeance. Landing unopposed at Southwark in September 1052 he immediately set out to expel all Normans from the kingdom.

Most travelled back to Normandy, but two, Osbern Pentecost and an ally called Hugh, went north to gain safety with Macbeth in Alba. Osbern had been the lord of a castle on the Anglo-Welsh border and would undoubtedly have been familiar with how to defend strategic locations. Macbeth was thus gaining useful assets, but why the two Normans chose to go to Alba is unknown.

Perhaps Macbeth had met them on his trip to Rome. Whatever the personal connection, Osbern's journey north is the first recorded evidence we have of Normans in Scotland. En route, the refugees may have sailed up to the Firth of Clyde before crossing through Strathclyde, then possibly Cumbrian territory, into Lothian. The south west of Scotland was most likely still not especially friendly to Macbeth, given its strong links to Duncan and Northumberland. The travellers would certainly have been noticed.

A Welcome, and then Business

If the two Normans and their families felt a sense of foreboding on reaching their new home it would not have been misplaced. No-one knew at the time, but their entrance signalled the beginning of the end of Gaelic rule in Alba. However, any dark thoughts would have receded with Macbeth's welcome. Crossing down to meet them perhaps at the River Allan they could have taken the Darn Walk (E2), a route used since Roman times, to one of Macbeth's fortified residences at Dunblane.

Here, they would have been royally entertained, drinking in the great hall and regaled with stories of the Kings of Scots. This would, of course, have ended with tales of Macbeth himself, *'the generous King of Fortrui'*[44]. Waking at the first hour of daylight, or Prime, the royal party might then have trekked north towards modern Dunning. Nearby lay the ancient fort of Duncrub and the wooden palace of Kenneth McAlpine at Forteviot (E3). After another night or two's rest the group might then have travelled north to Scone itself, on the banks of the Tay.

Then, it is reasonable to suggest, normal business would have resumed. Macbeth possibly toured his central kingdom with the Normans during the early part of the season. He may have introduced them to his existing fortifications running across the length of Alba. West to east these probably included Dundurn, Dunkeld, Dunsinane, Moredun and Dunnichen.

If time had allowed, the party might even have reached the spectacular fort of Dunnottar, near modern Stonehaven. Here, on the border of the northern and southern portions of Alba many famous battles had been fought. We can speculate that, this far north, Macbeth, standing proud, may have looked longingly towards his homeland of Moray before returning south, a confident ruler of the whole of Alba.

Realpolitik

Wherever the royal party was situated, word would soon have reached it of Earl Godwin's death in April 1053. Yet again, the scales of the balance had altered. Edward the Confessor was in complete control of what we term England, and one person close to his court planned trouble for Macbeth. We introduced him earlier as Malcolm, grandson of Crinan. He was now grown up and a protégé of Edward.

Malcolm was also known as 'Canmore'[45], and we might assume from his lordship of Corby, in Northamptonshire, that he understood the Old English tongue. It seems the son of Duncan now used this to good political effect, as he would become Macbeth's Achilles' Heel. Macbeth himself, having returned to Moray to avenge his own father many years earlier, probably understood the mind of Malcolm Canmore, and the importance of his southern contacts. So the alarming news that arrived the following year, in 1054, was probably not unexpected. Malcolm Canmore and his relative, Earl Siward of Northumbria, were marching north to invade Alba.

Pieces of a Jigsaw

There are many differing views as to why this invasion actually took place. It has even been proposed that a different Malcolm, from the kingdom of Cumbria, accompanied Siward on the expedition. We believe that two versions stand the reality test.

The first is that Edward the Confessor, understanding fully that strong Norman and Scandinavian factions were coveting his succession, wanted regime change in Alba.[46] By helping to install Malcolm Canmore on the throne, someone Edward thought would act as a puppet king, his hand would be strengthened in the escalating international political arena. This needed Earl Siward, who had reversed sides in 1052 by backing Godwin's return to England, to agree to Edward's request; to help place Malcolm Canmore on the throne of Alba.

An alternative scenario is that Siward himself was increasing looking to expand his influence to the north and west[47]. There was a strong Northumbrian influence on the Kingdom of Cumbria and Malcolm Canmore's own father had once ruled there. With this in mind, the driver for the 1054 invasion could have been Siward's desire to take full control of Cumbria whilst Edward the Confessor was busy in the south dealing with Godwin's son.

If Siward helped Malcolm Canmore to take the throne of Alba from Macbeth, then Siward might hold sway in Cumbria with a friendly King Malcolm overseeing the troublesome northern border. Both views are plausible, but there is a third.

In 1054 Malcolm Canmore would have been in his 20s. For most of his life he had lived in exile. Just like Macbeth, Malcolm had witnessed how to influence people and gain power. Almost mirroring Macbeth's own situation, Malcolm could have been driven by the desire to avenge the death of his father, Duncan, and reclaim what he saw as his birthright. It is highly likely, therefore, that Malcolm himself had persuaded both Edward and Siward to help him in this enterprise. Any agreement would have promised rewards for all parties.

Invasion Force

When the raiding season began in 1054, Siward and Malcolm headed north with an invasion force to try and overthrow Macbeth. The assembled army was large enough to merit mention in contemporary texts in both England and Ireland.[48]

Travelling by land and sea, this body would have comprised of a mixture of foot-soldiers, cavalry and seamen. Elite Huscarls provided by Edward the Confessor also marched north, as well as bowmen. The overall size of the army is unknown, but a safe estimate might be that it numbered between five to ten thousand men.[49] These warriors would have invariably been accompanied by a large train of equipment, supplies and camp followers, attracted by the potential plunder to be seized from the Kingdom of Alba.

The most obvious route northwards would have been to follow the north east coastline into Lothian. As the army crossed the river Tweed the men were no doubt reminded by their leaders of the cost of the Battle of Carham, in 1018. We can imagine that, for any unfortunate inhabitants who lived along the way, this passage would not have ended soon enough.

Accompanying the march, seagoing ships would have stayed close to the shore. Only when the land detachments reached the south western edges of the Firth of Forth would the ships have departed. This was to prepare to land supplies further north, probably in Tayside near the small port of Dundee. Meanwhile, the land army would have continued marching towards Stirling. At this location they would have had to cross the same tracks through the salt marshes that the Norman Knights had followed the year before.

Once across, we presume unopposed, a few days of hard marching would have brought them directly to Scone itself. This was the visible centre of power in Alba. Today, driving along the same route from Durham to Perth takes around five hours. In 1054, it would have taken at least four weeks, probably more, for Siward's army to reach Scone.

Fight or Flee

Macbeth had two options, either to fight or to flee. He chose the former, even though he may not have had too much time to prepare. A very quick muster would in all likelihood have resulted in most available men being summoned from Fife and Angus. Perhaps some loyal supporters from Moray even managed to join the royal army.

General historical thought has been that Macbeth's force was not as large as Siward's. It is true that, in an age when energy depended on human or animal muscle, to deprive all physical resources from a farmstead would have risked a bad season. At worst this meant starvation. A balance may have been required to try and obtain the best of both worlds. On the other hand, against such a large invading force this would inevitably have required Macbeth to summon every available man, with the associated human trauma this entailed.

Faced with such a direct assault on his rule it seems that Macbeth wasn't content to rely on guerrilla tactics. Indeed, it appears that he chose a strategy that might stop the invaders in their tracks. This meant battle, and so a battleground had to be chosen that would give his men the best advantage. The site most historians accept as the location for the showdown was near Dunsinane Hill (E4). Given its position in the very heart of Alba, less than eight miles from Scone, this was a high risk strategy. Perhaps there was no choice to be made?

Driving north from Perth, Dunsinane is reached by passing through the small village of Collace, now an oasis of calm. A walk to the summit of Dunsinane Hill is worthwhile, and the view from the top commanding. To the north stretches the high ground of the Cairngorms, the mountain barrier that still shields Moray and the north east from the rest of the country. Any force advancing from the south could be spotted for miles, as could enemy ships landing in the Tay valley.

There had been a hill fort at the top of Dunsinane for many centuries. Even if it had been neglected in Macbeth's time it would still have been an obvious place for safely billeting both the local population and a defending army. To storm such a substantial defensive position on the top of a 1,000 foot high hill would have been energy sapping. We can imagine Macbeth standing silently, in 1054, watching the invaders assemble on the plains of Gowrie below.

Writing in the 14th century John of Fordun[50] tells us that this invasion caused turmoil amongst the local population, who were unsure who to support. This is an intriguing thought given the proximity of Dunsinane to Dunkeld. Sited not far to the north-west, Dunkeld was Malcolm Canmore's ancestral home, and most likely sympathetic to the returning son of Duncan. If reinforcements had marched from here to join up with Malcolm and Siward then they would have passed through Birnam Wood!

The Battle of Dunsinane

There is so much conjecture, but the sources[51] state that on 27 July 1054, on the festival of the Seven Sleepers, the two armies faced each other. Someone had to make the first move. It is not unrealistic to imagine Macbeth looking around at his people, secure and watered by the hilltop well, but lacking major food supplies for a lengthy siege. This would have made a decision to attack first relatively easy. Perhaps shouting out the same battle cry used against the father, Macbeth could have launched a downhill charge against the son. The ranks of massed invaders below made the implication clear. Once again, it was all or nothing.

Hand to hand fighting is difficult for most modern citizens to comprehend. Cocooned from violence we cannot even imagine the thoughts of those involved. Surrounded by confusion and noise, wretched cries for help, bone splintering on steel, the inhabitants of Alba were fighting for their lives and those of their families too. For the victors the spoils of war would have consisted of cattle, food and human beings, often led away to a life of slavery. Looking down today on the sleepy village of Collace, it is difficult to imagine the 11th century carnage.

One source[52] speaks of 3,000 men of Alba slain. The invaders didn't escape lightly either, suffering 1,500 dead. This massive casualty list included Siward's own son as well as Osbern the Norman, who had come to Alba to work with Macbeth. The outcome, however, was not decisive. It seems that Macbeth departed the field with Alba effectively split in two, and there was no real winner. We can only assume that Macbeth realised at some point that his men were being overcome, so he left the field at the last minute and headed north.

One route Macbeth may have taken was through the Spittal of Glenshee via modern Braemar. This would have made for a speedy, but difficult, journey direct to Moray. Here, on reaching home territory, we believe that Macbeth could have consolidated his position and planned revenge. After the battle, Malcolm Canmore was supposedly crowned King of Alba at Scone. Macbeth's flight and Malcolm's ceremony may or may not have happened. What was relevant was that Macbeth still lived, and he still ruled over a large area.

Aftermath

The outcome of the Battle of the Seven Sleepers has long been debated. Some say that Macbeth held firm in Moray protected by the formidable barrier of the Mounth. Others speculate that he regained control of Alba as far south as the Firth of Forth, whilst Malcolm ruled in Lothian and Cumbria. As ever, supporting facts are few, although we do know that Siward returned home relatively quickly with much plunder.[53]

Siward's departure would have weakened the invading force, effectively leaving Macbeth and Malcolm in a vacuum. Macbeth had ruled Alba successfully for 14 years, so it is not unreasonable to suggest that he retained much support from the Alban nobles. This might have been a case of 'better the devil you know', as opposed to a new ruler who had not been brought up in Alba, and who had close links to Northumbria and England.

If Macbeth received this support then, along with his need to retain respect, it would lead us to surmise that he would have continued to fight. With this thought in mind, there are two major physical barriers in Scotland, the Firth-Clyde isthmus and the

Mounth. It would be a safe bet to assume that, after the battle, Malcolm controlled the southern lands below the former whilst Macbeth held the lands north of the latter. Immediately after the battle Malcolm would also have held the territory from Scone southwards.

If we try to place ourselves inside Malcolm's head then it seems unlikely, assuming a long term goal to conquer, that he would have wanted to cede any captured territories. Malcolm could also call on family support from the area around Dunkeld. So, if we assume that Macbeth fought on, then there is a good probability that the heart of Alba, from Fife and Strathearn through to Angus and the Mearns, may have ended up as disputed lands between the two factions.

Long Mysterious Years

Disputed territories would have been a nightmare for local inhabitants, more so if they had suffered losses at the Battle of the Seven Sleepers. We have no evidence for what might have happened over the course of the next three years, but if Macbeth the warrior king fought on to regain land he may have resorted to guerrilla tactics. This means that the population of some parts of Alba would have had to cope with continual skirmishing. During this period, violence would have been as constant as the sun rising each morning.

Raiding with his personal war band, who had pledged themselves to their leader, Macbeth's initial strikes from Moray might have been in Angus. His experienced and accomplished warriors would have been capable of planned and co-ordinated manoeuvres before retreating back to safe positions across the mountain passes.

If this were so, the Angus countryside then would have been fertile, but full of aggression. Today, it is fertile and peaceful, and the old Forfar road heads quietly north east from Dunsinane. After a while it takes you past the famous Glamis Castle (E5). There is no factual evidence of Macbeth having done anything here, although it is within raiding distance from the north.

Less than an hour's drive in this direction from Glamis is

Fettercairn. It lies at the base of a famous path across the Mounth at Cairn o'Mount (E6). This leads into the old province of Mar, bounded on its southern border by the river Dee. Beyond Mar lay the border lands of Moray. Standing at the top of Cairn o'Mount looking south the Angus plain is a tempting prize. If you turn north, you are looking towards another world.

Death of a King

The area north of the Mounth was where Macbeth met his death in 1057. As ever, there are numerous suggestions as to how this came about. Two stories are worth considering.

The conventional version echoes a local tradition[54] which says that in 1057 Macbeth had been raiding south of the Mounth and he returned north via the old Fir Mounth drove road. This is sited to the west of the modern B974 and even today is a remote and difficult walk. Supposedly, Macbeth then crossed the Dee into Mar at the ford of Craig Farrar. Meanwhile, a party led by Malcolm himself had been following Macbeth and they crossed the Mounth by the conventional route, roughly following the B974, arriving at Kincardine O'Neil (E7) a few miles to the east of Macbeth.

As Macbeth headed north east towards Moray the two groups met at Lumphanan (E8). Standing at the Peel of Lumphanan today, which is the site of a castle built after Macbeth's time, the place feels very remote. Back in 1057 it was a strategic doorway into Strathbogie, and would have been surrounded by low lying marsh and lochans.

Perhaps Macbeth's Stone, 200 yards to the south of the Peel, was where Macbeth made his last stand? Supposedly 17 years to the day since Macbeth had killed Malcolm's father in battle, the two protagonists came face to face. A warrior king to the last, we can imagine Macbeth turning at bay to face his pursuers, sounding his battle cry and charging toward his foe. The clash of swords would have rung out across the valley as the last Celtic King of Alba met his death in combat.

Another version of events[55] has Macbeth killed by Malcolm at

Lumphanan, but with Malcolm approaching either from the north or the north east, possibly with Viking allies. This scenario is plausible given that an alliance with the Earls of Orkney was something that could have made strategic sense to Malcolm. This would be later enhanced by his marriage to Earl Thorfinn's widow, Ingibiorg. If this supposition was true, then Macbeth might have regained power in central Alba and was travelling north to defend his kingdom.

Lulach

This latter suggestion might also fit with the kingship passing to his stepson Lulach. Sources[56] say that after Macbeth died Lulach, the son of Gruoch and Gilla Comgáin, assumed the kingship of Alba. For Lulach to have been inaugurated at Scone then many believe that the Moray kindred must have held sway south of the Mounth. It seems that even on Macbeth's death there are major questions left unanswered, befitting a man whose real life has been veiled for almost 1,000 years.

Most historians accept that after Macbeth died Lulach reigned for a matter of months before being killed by Malcolm in March 1058. Others believe, based on dates taken from the Irish annals, that Macbeth outlived Lulach, although Lulach may have been passed the throne beforehand. We will never know the truth. Lulach was of royal pedigree, but we shouldn't necessarily assume that, in a time of potential conflict, Kings could only be inaugurated if they managed to get to Scone.

There is much to gain from travelling north to where Lulach met his death. Heading out from Lumphanan you enter the territory of Strathbogie. Entering the region of Essie, near Mossat (E9) you are on the edge of no-man's land, the ancient boundary region between the north east and the kingdom of Moray. This is a haunting and lonely place. Parking on the main road next to a local fish farm you can look around the wooded hills. Somewhere hidden from view stands Lulach's Stone. According to local legend this is where Lulach was slain by Malcolm through treachery.

To understand the geographical significance of the site you must continue travelling across the Garioch to arrive at Mortlach (E10), sited on the ancient Moray border. Once you have taken this journey it is not too far removed to speculate that, having killed Macbeth the previous year, once the winter frost had thawed Malcolm offered terms to Lulach, who was based in Moray. Lulach could then have left Moray at Mortlach to meet with Malcolm at Essie. Here, he was brutally slain and consigned to history as a nonentity.

For this scenario to have occurred, Malcolm would have had to come up from the south, most probably without Viking help. Indeed, if the so called Aberdeen Charters[57] are believed, and if they do relate to Malcolm Canmore, then he made provisions to the church at Mortlach, but only after defeating Vikings there. Perhaps the defeat of the Moray regime with Lulach's death offered an opportunity for the Earls of Orkney to exploit. If Malcolm subsequently put down further trouble in the north, then ongoing negotiations with Vikings may have ended with his marriage to Ingiebiorg, Thorfinn's widow.

The End of Many Things

Whatever really happened, Macbeth and his stepson were dead and the undoubted ruler of Alba was Malcolm, son of Duncan. His knowledge of English customs and administration would bequeath a dynasty that changed the face of Scotland. No-one knew this back then, but the momentum for change would become visible later in his reign when Malcolm married Margaret, sister of Edgar, the last male line of the House of Wessex.

An era in Scottish history, which had begun with Kenneth MacAlpin, finally ended in 1057. The penultimate chapter had opened in 1034 when Malcolm II, the last of the MacAlpin Kings died with no male heir. His successor Duncan claimed the throne through the female line, but he was weak. After disastrous defeats by Vikings and Northumbrians Macbeth, the powerful Mormaer of Moray took the throne of Alba in battle.

In this final chapter Macbeth led Alba for 17 years giving stability and '*productive seasons*'.[58] His prowess was revered and we are told his subjects thought him a '*generous King*'[59] who brought prosperity to his lands. We have to approach characters in history very carefully. Macbeth was a strong leader who has been unfairly maligned by later myth. An interesting and contemporary contrast is Edward the Confessor, an arguably weaker king made great by the same methods.

History, as ever, is written by the victors. At his death, Macbeth was old for his time, but we believe his passing in 1057 would have been mourned by his people. As with all Kings of Alba, we are told his body was carried to its final resting place in Iona. Macbeth's last great journey would probably have taken him back through Moray and then down along the Great Glen, perhaps to the beach at Dores where our story began.

Befitting his status, Macbeth's body would have passed by boat down through the lochs of the Great Glen until it reached Iona (F1). There, on a tiny island set in the Atlantic, buffeted by winds and rains, lay the monastery of St Columba, a shining light in the dark. This was indeed a fitting place for Macbeth to lie at rest, the last great Celtic King of Scotland.

The Beginning of Countless Tales

IMAGINING THE PAST

The sounds of south London filtered into the small room, wrestling with shafts of light for the playwright's attention. Neither roused him. He was lost in a distant world, centuries past. Trembling with anticipation he placed his pen on the parchment. Soon, a monstrous new character would be born. The audience would have their fill again!

CHAPTER 7

The Beginning of Countless Tales

THE MODERN WORLD uses a massive range of channels with which to communicate. Even so, all depend on basic human senses such as sight and sound. But this still gives us myriads of opportunities for misunderstanding, especially when opinions might be wrongly perceived as facts. Add to the mix the ability of an average human being to only remember about 25 per cent of what is heard, and it would seem we have an innate ability to misinterpret.

First Stories

The earliest tales of Macbeth would have begun when he was alive. As only a few people could write in the 11th century, Macbeth's exploits would have been transmitted orally in Gaelic, as entertainment. Seated around a great drinking hall with his war band, Macbeth may have listened to a bard, or poet, regaling the assembled throng with warriors' deeds. These would then have been spread by word of mouth, much as we discuss topical issues today.

As the King, Macbeth's deeds would have been enhanced through *praise poems* such as those possibly based in the *Prophecy of Berchan*.[60] This work takes its name from an Irish Saint, although it was probably written by a number of different individuals in the 11th century. Given both the contemporaneous and the sympathetic nature of the material, it is likely that parts of this poem were delivered in front of Macbeth himself, *the red, tall, golden haired one* whose reign brought Alba prosperity.

In contrast, Duncan is not given a similar treatment in the *Prophecy of Berchan*. However, in another 11th century series of poems, the *Duan Albanach*,[61] he is described as '*handsome*' and of '*lively aspect*'. Although limited in extent, both these works highlight that even in the 11th century there were different versions of character analysis emerging for both Macbeth and Duncan.

Outwith these sources, and the annal records, we found no other reference to Macbeth until the 13th century with the *Verse Chronicle*.[62] This is basically a king list which refers to Macbeth's reign as bringing '*fruitful seasons*' to Alba. Importantly, it also amplifies annal statements that Macbeth took the kingship without any authority.

A Changing World

A century later, John Fordun, who died in the 1370s, wrote a *Chronicle of the Scottish People*. He is said to have researched many documents, interviewed people and travelled extensively to see where events had happened on the ground. His account of Macbeth is significant, as he is now characterised not only a usurper, but a murderer and a tyrant as well. As part of the developing myth, MacDuff the Thane of Fife also makes a first appearance in the story.

We have to place Fordun in context. He lived in the era after Bannockburn, with continuing English aspirations for control north of the border. Fordun was more than likely trying to emphasise the traditions of a rightful Scottish kingship ruling over a rightful Scottish nation. Unfortunately for Macbeth, 300 years after he lived Fordun positioned him as an illegitimate ruler. This set a continuing trend that was taken up at the start of the 15th century by Andrew Wyntoun.

Writing in his *Original Chronicle of Scotland*, Wyntoun moved creative elaboration a stage further. Not only did Macbeth, the Thane of Cromarty, murder Duncan, but Macbeth was also the son of the devil. What this meant was that Macbeth could only be killed by someone of unnatural birth. Wyntoun also introduced three weird sisters speaking to Macbeth in a dream. Macbeth is told about his royal destiny and that he will remain undefeated until Birnam Wood comes to Dunsinane Hill.

There are many elements from ancient folklore, such as the

recurrence of the number three, females who prophesise about the destinies of men and stories involving woods, in Wyntoun's treatment. He also wrote at a time when witchcraft trials were prevalent in Western Europe. Without doubt, Wyntoun's writing placed Macbeth's story further away from reality. The Macbeth legend was moving into fictional space, although one contemporary 15th century writer, Walter Bower, left out aspects of the supernatural in his *Scotichronicon*. This work was a continuation of Fordun's *Chronicle of the Scottish People* and, although generally unfavourable to Macbeth, did concede that his reign was prosperous.

The 16th Century

Moving into the first half of the 16th century we reach the colourful accounts written by Hector Boece in his *History of the Scottish People*. Notable refinements to the Macbeth story from Boece are the invention of Banquo as the Thane of Lochaber and the description of Lady Macbeth as a power-hungry queen. It is now Gruoch who apparently compelled her husband to murder King Duncan in his bed!

These and other considerations were picked up by Ralph Holinshed who published *The Chronicles of England, Scotland and Ireland* in 1577, and then again in 1587. This work really introduced the Macbeth story to an English audience and, importantly, it listed Banquo as a direct relation to James VI of Scotland. James had come to the Scottish throne in 1567 and, in time, he would become James I of England. So, the stage was now set, as it were, for the most famous version of Macbeth, by a certain William Shakespeare, master playwright.

Writing a Play

But what does it take to write a great play? Well, first of all you need to understand that a play is a story told in public. With this in mind you then need to figure out who the characters will be, and what events will happen to them. Great plays introduce memorable characters, and the story develops through the characters who embrace conflict and unknown consequences.

Unlike a novel, where the story usually takes place inside the mind of a lead character, or a film script, which is a story told in pictures, a play takes place on a stage. Within this enclosed physical space the playwright must be aware not only how the play sounds, but also how the characters look and how they move. Everything that happens must be justified. Once all of these essential ingredients are mixed together the audience then eavesdrops, listening in to the lives of the characters.

The key action of a play occurs within the language of the playwright. From this the needs, dreams, desires and fears of the characters are all brought vividly to life. It is for this ability that William Shakespeare is undoubtedly revered as one of the greatest dramatists in the world. So who was he, and why did he end up writing about Macbeth?

The Playwright

William Shakespeare was born in April 1564, almost 500 years after Macbeth died at Lumphanan. Shakespeare was the third of eight children and in later life his father held the position of Mayor of Stratford-upon-Avon. This is where William grew up and it was here, at the age of 18, that he married Anne Hathaway, a local farmer's daughter.

Although Shakespeare lived much closer to our own times than he did to Macbeth's, there is still much we do not know. Some say that Shakespeare had loved another woman but married Anne, eight years his senior, because she was pregnant with his first child. Who can tell? Perhaps it is easier to try and describe the England of Elizabeth I, who was queen when William Shakespeare was born.

Sixteenth century people lived and died, toiled and loved in the same way we do today. But they differed in a number of respects. For example, life expectancy only reached into the lower 40s. This was the era of plague. Childhood, if survived, was often short before a severe working life began. Attendance at church was probably compulsory and, for most of society, the idea of marriage for love was wishful thinking. Perhaps this is why Shakespeare left Stratford in 1587, to become an actor and playwright in London.

The Audience

In the latter part of the 16th century London probably housed a population in the order of 200,000, a tenfold rise since Macbeth's time. It was the growing capital of England and, back then, lay mainly north of the river Thames stretching from Smithfield up to Shoreditch, then reaching across to Clerkenwell before heading south through Holborn to run along the Strand down to Westminster. Southwark lay on the southern shore opposite London Bridge.

In a basic sense, Elizabethan plays might be compared to early Hollywood movies. Theatres were in their infancy and the bulk of the 16th century audience would have been ordinary commoners who had to pay to see the shows. Their increasing demand for entertainment meant, that in Shakespeare's time, entrepreneurial businessmen were soon opening theatres across the city.

The plays themselves were scripted relatively quickly, before being performed only a limited number of times. Once their product lifecycle was spent, they were replaced by another play. Amidst this background Shakespeare quickly established his credentials. By 1599 he had became the joint proprietor of the Globe Theatre, sited south of the river Thames in the sprawling estate of Southwark.

The entrance fee to get into the Globe would have been around one penny. A full house capacity would have been in the order of 2,000 people. The proximity of the audience to the stage will have made the performances very intimate and all of the actors were male, even for the female parts.

Shakespeare's plays were probably first performed in the early 1590s, but they weren't published until after his death in 1623. We aren't sure of the original dates of the plays, although it is generally accepted that the *Tragedie of Macbeth* was written in 1605 and first performed in 1606.

Placing the origin of Shakespeare's *Macbeth* in context, Queen Elizabeth of England had died in 1603. Unlike the 11th-century rules of succession, kings and queens in Shakespeare's time followed the principle of primogeniture, with the first born of the ruling monarch taking the throne. Having no children of her own Elizabeth was followed by her closest relative, her cousin, King James of Scotland.

With the crowns of Scotland and England unified, it's easy to understand why Scottish themes might have been of interest to people in southern England. A number of Scottish plays were written although Shakespeare's *Tragedie of Macbeth* is one of the few that survives. Theatre companies weren't allowed to refer to living rulers or directly address contemporary religious issues, so playwrights such as Shakespeare addressed topical issues by incorporating them into historical dramas.

King James himself supported the Globe's band of actors, who called themselves the *King's men*. Building on this link, some say that the *Tragedie of Macbeth* was written specifically for the royal visit of Christian IV of Denmark, James' brother in law, in 1606. If so, it is highly likely that Shakespeare pandered to his monarch when writing the *Tragedie of Macbeth* by making sure that, in the subject matter, James's personal interests were well to the fore. These included demonology and witchcraft, and the rightful rule of kings through appropriate succession. James himself had even written a number of treatises on these subjects, possibly inspired by major events of the period which included some high profile witchcraft trials and the Gunpowder Plot in 1605.

What is written must be so!

Although we cannot understand the specific origins of Shakespeare's play, he clearly wrote it within the context of his own times. A contemporary rival, Ben Jonson, said that Shakespeare was *the soul of his age*.[63] This is a strong clue that Shakespeare's content probably did capture current issues before innovatively re-distributing them to the masses within a specific historic setting.

The main source for The *Tragedie of Macbeth* was probably the second edition of Holinshead's *The Chronicles of England, Scotland and Ireland* published in 1587. Shakespeare didn't only draw on this account of the real Macbeth, he embellished the story by mixing in other tales for dramatic effect. Hence, the original story of a certain Donald killing a King Duff in a castle was turned into Macbeth killing King Duncan in a castle. There is also the character of Banquo, invented centuries earlier, being introduced as the founder of the Stewart line, of which James I was the latest.

This heady brew was then stirred further by Shakespeare's own imagination. A good example of this is the age of King Duncan. He seems an old man in the play, rather than a contemporary who had grown up with Macbeth. The end result is a truly entertaining story about a man's ambition and treachery, and his inability to cope with the outcome. As a testament to the real Macbeth it is grossly unfair, but then the real Macbeth wasn't Shakespeare's intended audience.

Beyond Shakespeare

Since Shakespeare's play was first performed ongoing generations have been intrigued by Macbeth's fictional character. This interest has flowered with increased access to mass communication channels. As a vehicle, the play is relatively short, mixing strong and dramatic, but flawed, characters with the supernatural. It has consistently drawn the very best acting talent to its stage, even with its reputation as the *Scottish play*.

The acting profession is used to superstition and some in the trade will not mention Macbeth's name within a theatre, as this is meant to bring bad luck. We do not know why. Some have said it was because many theatre companies would, in times of financial hardship, put on plays they knew the public would come to see. If this was the case, then the *Tragedie of Macbeth*, as a staple crowd puller, might have been performed to revive cash flows. Afterwards, if the required monies hadn't been gained, then there was a good chance that the Macbeth play could have been the last performance before the theatre company folded.

Others believe that the legend of the Scottish play is related to the supernatural element. Whatever the truth, there have been many grave events linked to performances of Macbeth. In one legend, the actor playing Macbeth reputedly killed the actor playing Duncan onstage with a real dagger in an adaptation from 1672. But perhaps the worst was the New York Astor Theatre riot of 1849. Trouble began when the theatre company announced that the British tragedian, William Macready, would play Macbeth instead of the local New York favourite Edwin Forrest. These two thespians also had a personal history and this happened at a time when New Yorkers held strong views against foreigners.

The city seethed and when Macready opened on 7 May he was pelted with rotten eggs. He was persuaded to continue the run and on 10 May he stepped back onto the stage to play Macbeth. At exactly the same time, Forrest opened up as Spartacus, not more than half a mile away on Broadway. Supporters of both actors, polarised into American versus English sentiments, filled the streets and as Macready began Act 2 a riot broke out. Over 10,000 people were involved, a scene more suited to the real Battle of Dunsinane, and in the aftermath there were 31 people dead.

Enduring Appeal

The New York riot partly explains the continuing appeal of Shakespeare's Macbeth. As well as having great characterisation and plot, the play has been constantly converted and repackaged to blend into contemporary society, whatever the period, wherever the place and whatever the media.

In the romantic era of the 19th century Macbeth adorned oil paintings and spawned operas. Modern novelists have retold the story in their own fashion, including Nigel Tranter's *Macbeth the King* (1978) and Catherine Well's *The Stones of Destiny* (2007). Poems abound about Macbeth and Lady Macbeth whilst a series of graphic novels, published by Classical Comics, vividly brings the Shakespearean character to life in modern English and original text too.

There is a long list of cinematic versions of Macbeth dating from the silent movies. Stand-outs perhaps include Orson Welles's *Macbeth* (1948), Akiro Kurosawa's *Kumonosu-Ju* (1957), where the action is transposed to medieval Japan, and Roman Polanski's bruising *Macbeth* (1971). Other types of film based on Shakepeare's Macbeth include Ken Hughes's *Joe Macbeth* (1955) and Geoffrey Wright's *Macbeth* (2006) based in Melbourne, both set amongst gangsters.

The cultural diversity of Shakespeare's Macbeth is astounding, and general Shakespeare database collections of note include the complete works of Shakespeare online at MIT[64] and the Canadian Adaptations of Shakespeare Project,[65] the latter devoted to the systematic exploration and documentation of the ways in which Shakespeare has been adapted into a national, multicultural theatrical practice.

There will be many variants of *The Tragedy of Macbeth* yet to come, including home-made versions as befitting the YouTube generation. As this book is being written there are literally thousands of clips available on YouTube highlighted on typing in 'Macbeth', including finger puppets and Lego characters!

During the summer of 2007 the National Theatre of Scotland

staged an event in the ruins of Elgin Cathedral, allegedly on the very spot where King Duncan died in 1040. This large scale, open air project brought Shakespeare's myth home to Moray, where the real man had been born. The ambitious performance was presented not only by a professional cast, but incorporated multimedia work and featured members of the local schools and community cast as a Chorus. The community aspect revived an ancient hero, who had previously been forgotten by the majority of the local inhabitants.

A Final Thought

Entrancing stories always begin with a lead character facing a crisis that turns his or her world upside down. The ensuing dramatic need then drives the action as the crisis is solved. Most lead characters are likable and virtuous, but William Shakespeare wrote a tragic play for a fictional Macbeth which, by a combination of personal failing and not coping with the circumstance, ends in disaster.

That the appeal of this particular anti-hero reaches right up to the modern day is a testament to Shakespeare's dramatic skills, allied to the subsequent growth of a massive 'Shakespeare Macbeth' brand identity. This has left an indelible mark on the world.

The value of the media Macbeth lies in Shakespeare's fictional character and the themes of temptation and ambition. The allure is simple. Someone took something that wasn't theirs and ultimately lost it in an exciting climax. The moral order was therefore restored, even against the will of Lady Macbeth, the scheming woman behind the man.

The double act of Shakespeare's Macbeth and his woman is powerful entertainment. So much so that Macbeth's memory is dominated by Shakespeare's fabrications. These have spawned a stream of cultural production that is most unfair to the real Macbeth and Gruoch, a successful warrior king and his respected queen. The real man led his kingdom at a pivotal time in its development and his actions gained him respect in his own time, even amongst his enemies.

Although Shakespeare's original play is masterful, it must be placed in context as a tipping point that has subsequently masked the likely train of events that led Macbeth to become a successful and highly important King of Alba.

Perhaps the real Macbeth's time has come again?

Postscript

IMAGING THE PAST

Gruoch, no longer Queen of Alba and no longer mother to a king, stood on the shoreline of the tiny island of Iona and prepared to leave. She had spoken silent farewells to her dead husband and son and ensured that the monks would say prayers for their souls. Then she had released her husband's followers – those few who remained alive – from any obligation to her, only urging them to keep in mind their king when they told stories of Alba to their children and their children's children. 'Remember, he was a real man; the real Macbeth, King of Alba.'

On the Trail of the Real Macbeth

WE HOPE THAT the story of the real Macbeth has inspired you to find out more. You can use the following appendices to do so and come and join us on the trail. We are sure that there is more to find out.

As well as notes from each chapter we have included indexes of people's names (with a brief explanation of who the main characters in the story were) and the main places mentioned in the book. In addition there is a chronology of the main events described in the book, together with a selected reading list.

Finally there is a touring itinerary that you can use as the basis of your own personal exploration of the places and landscapes associated with Macbeth. The itinerary provides links back to the story we tell in this book so you can re-read it as you travel in Macbeth's footsteps.

Appendix A

Notes

WHILE THIS IS not an academic textbook we have included some references that may help you follow up aspects of Macbeth's story in more detail if you wish.

INTRODUCTION

1   The Mounth is the range of hills forming a ridge of the Grampian Mountains on the southern edge of Strathdee. The word 'Mounth' is a corruption of the Gaelic 'monadh'.

CHAPTER ONE

2   See Aitchison, N., *Macbeth: Man and Myth*, Stroud, 2000, p. 5

3   Mark Nicholls, *Scotland Magazine*, Issue 32, 2007 citing Dingwall as the birthplace of Macbeth, and see www.clandavidsonusa.com et al

4   *Annals of Ulster* a.s. 1020.6 in Anderson, A.O. *Early sources of Scottish History*, Edinburgh, 1922

5   See Woolf, A., *From Pictland to Alba 789–1070*, Edinburgh, 2007, pp. 240–242 for a discussion on Moray dynastic links

6   Delaney, F., *The Celts*, London, 1989, pp. 17 and 64, and Davies, N, *Europe: A History*, Oxford, 1996, p221

7   See Aitchison, N., *The Picts and the Scots at War*, Stroud, 2003, Chapter 3 for discussion on military organisation

8   Boece, *Scotorum Historiae* 2: p. 143

9   See *Annals of Tigernach* T1020.8 www.ucc.ie/celt/published

10   See Aitchison, N., *Macbeth: Man and Myth*, Stroud, 2000,
     p. 111 discussing Andrew Wyntoun's *Orygynale Cronykil*,
     which mentions the Thanage of Cromarty in the Black Isle
     in relation to a conversation with three weird sisters,
     Wyntoun 4: p. 273

CHAPTER TWO

11   Oram, R., *Kings and Queens of Scotland*, Stroud, 2006,
     p. 45

12   As with so many dates in medieval history, the date of the
     battle of Carham is open to dispute. See Duncan, A.A.M.,
     The battle of Carham, 1018, Scottish Historical Review,
     55:1=159 (1976) p. 20–28

13   Woolf, A., *From Pictland to Alba 789–1070*, Edinburgh,
     2007, p. 228

14   Woolf, A., *From Pictland to Alba 789–1070*, Edinburgh,
     2007, p. 244

15   See for instance Hudson, B.T., *Canute and the Scottish
     Kings*, English Historical Review 1992 pp350–360 and
     Lynch, M. (ed) *Oxford Companion to Scottish History*,
     Oxford, 2007, p. 402

16   Now topped by a 17th century Doocot, the mound is also
     an excellent vantage point from which to survey the site of
     the Battle of Auldearn, fought in 1645

CHAPTER THREE

17   From Earl Thorfinn's poet – or skald – Arnor who wrote
     '*Unto Thorfinn, Ravens Feeder, armies had to yield
     obedience.*' quoted in Crawford, B., *Scandinavian Scotland*,
     Leicester, 1987, p. 75

18 Palsson, H. and Ewards, P. trans. *Orkneyinga Saga*, Harmondsworth, 1981 p38 and also Gray, *Sutherland and Caithness in Saga Time*: http://infomotions.com/ etexts/gutenberg/dirs/1/5/8/5/15856/15856.htm

19 *Orkneyinga Saga*, p. 51

20 *Orkneyinga Saga*, p. 54

21 *Orkneyinga Saga*, p. 51

22 The *Orkneyinga Saga* only mentions the name Karl Hundasson when describing the Scottish King who fought with Thorfinn over Caithness and Sutherland. Some historians believe that Karl was Macbeth whilst others believe that Karl was Duncan.

23 See Marianus Scottus, *Chronicle*, 1040, 'Duncan, the King of Scotland, was killed on the nineteenth day of the Kalends of September by his earl, Macbeth, Findláech's son' and *Prose and Verse Chronicles inserted in the Chronicle of Melrose*, 1034, 'Macbeth, son of Findláech, struck him a mortal wound. The king died at Elgin.' Anderson, A.O. *Early sources of Scottish History*, Edinburgh, 1922

24 Aitchison, N., *Macbeth: Man and Myth*, Stroud, 2000, p. 62

25 A local legend has it that Duncan was buried near a well in Inverness, not far from Auldcastle Road, but other sources imply he was finally laid to rest in Iona.

26 To establish primacy as a ruler by both gaining the assent of the ruling class and church, thereby reducing the risk of an opponent.

27 See *The Prophecy of Berchan*, 'Scotland will be brimful west and east during the reign of the furious red one.'

CHAPTER FOUR

28 The Stone of Destiny returned to Scotland in 1996 and is now housed in Edinburgh Castle in the care of Historic Scotland.

29 Duncan, A.A.M., *Scotland: The Making of the Kingdom*, Edinburgh, 1975, p. 115

30 Driscoll, S., *Alba: the Gaelic Kingdom of Scotland* AD *800–1124*, Edinburgh, 2002, p. 37

31 Aitchison, N., *Macbeth: Man and Myth*, Stroud, 2000, p71

32 See, for instance, Oram, R., *David I: The King who made Scotland*, Stroud 2004, p. 22 and Wolf, A,. *From Pictland to Alba*, Edinburgh, 2007, p. 265

33 Anderson, A.O., *Early sources of Scottish History*, Edinburgh, 1922, p. 583

34 Quoted in Aitchison, N., *Macbeth: Man and Myth*, Stroud, 2000, p. 72

35 Adapted from Woolf, A., *From Pictland to Alba*, Edinburgh, 2007, p. 346

36 See Anderson, A.O., *Early sources of Scottish History*, Edinburgh, 1922, p. 601

37 Marsden J., *Alba of the Ravens*, London, 1997, p. 193

38 See www.bookofdeer.co.uk for information about the Book of Deer project

39 Barrow, G.W.S. *Feudal Britain* London, 1956, p. 138

CHAPTER FIVE

40 See Anderson, A.O. *Early sources of Scottish History* Edinburgh, 1922, p. 588

41 The Rule of St Benedict is a book of precepts or rules written by St Benedict, designed to govern communities of monks living under the authority of an abbot. St Benedict is sometimes referred to as the founder of Western monasticism.

42 The five Patriarchs were in effect senior Bishops who were regarded as having precedence over others. The five were the Bishops of Rome, Byzantium, Alexandria, Jerusalem and Antioch.

CHAPTER SIX

43 Schama, S. *A. History of Britain* London, 2000, p. 77–82

44 See the *Prophecy of Berchan* pp.193–195, translated by Hudson, B.T. 1996: 91 and quoted in Aitchison, N. *Macbeth: Man and Myth*, Stroud, 2000, p. 101

45 'Canmore' is generally thought to have meant 'big head' or 'long neck'. Burton, J., *The History of Scotland*, New Edition, Volume 1, p350, Edinburgh 1876 states: '*Malcolm the son of Duncan is known as Malcolm III, but still better perhaps by his characteristic name of Canmore, said to come from the Celtic 'Caenmohr', meaning 'great head'.*'

46 See for instance Aitchison, N. *Macbeth: Man and Myth*, Stroud, 2000, p. 85

47 See for instance Woolf, A. *From Pictland to Alba* Edinburgh, 2007, p. 263

48 *Anglo Saxon Chronicle* s.a. 1054, D text www.britannia.com/history and also *Annals of Ulster* a.s. 1054.6 www.ucc.ie/celt/published

49 See Aitchison, N. *The Picts and the Scots at War* Stroud, 2003, Chapter 2 for earlier military estimates

50 Fordun, J *Chronicle of the Scottish Nation, Vol.2*, *Edinburgh, 1872.*

51 See *Anglo Saxon Chronicle, translation by M. Swanton, London 1996, 1054* D and C texts and *Annals of Tigernach* T1054.5 www.ucc.ie/celt/published and the *Chronicle of Melrose* which states *'in the year 1054, Siward, earl of the Northumbrians, by king Edward's command entered Scotland with a great army; fought a battle with the king of Scots, Macbeth, and put him to flight; and appointed Malcolm king, as the king had commanded.'* Anderson, A.O. *Early Sources of Scottish History* Edinburgh, 1922

52 See *Annals of Ulster* a.s. 1054.6 in Anderson, A.O. *Early Sources of Scottish History* Edinburgh, 1922

53 See *Anglo Saxon Chronicle* s.a. 1054, http://omacl.org/ Anglo/part5.html

54 Marren, P. *Grampian Battlefields*, Edinburgh, 1993, Chapter 4

55 Woolf, A. *From Pictland to Alba* Edinburgh, 2007, pp. 263–271

56 See Anderson, A.O. *Early Sources of Scottish History* Edinburgh, 1922 p. 603: the *Chronicle of the Kings of Scotland* says that *'Lulach the simpleton reigned for four months. And he was killed in Essie, in Strathbogie; and was buried in the island of Iona.'*

57 See Marren, P. *Grampian Battlefields*, Edinburgh, 1993, p. 40 and Woolf, A. *From Pictland to Alba* Edinburgh, 2007, p. 269 relating to the *Aberdeen Registrum*

58 See *The Verse Chronicle*, Kelly translation 'Macbeth was King of Scots for 17 years and in his reign there were fruitful seasons' and quoted in Aitchison, N. *Macbeth: Man and Myth*, Stroud, 2000, p. 106

59 See the *Prophecy of Berchan*, Hudson translation 'after slaughter of Gaels, after slaughter of Vikings, the generous King of Fortrui will take sovereignty.' and quoted in Aitchison, N. *Macbeth: Man and Myth*, Stroud, 2000, p. 101

CHAPTER SEVEN

60 *The Prophecy of Berchan* was written by a number of poets in the 11th century and only survives in later manuscripts. It is believed to contain segments of *praise poems* commissioned for individuals such as Macbeth.

61 The *Duan Albannach* is a history of Scottish Kings probably originally composed in Ireland in the 11th century.

62 The *Verse Chronicle* is a Scottish King list with annalistic entries probably composed in the reign of Alexander II (1214–1249).

63 Chambers, E.K. *William Shakespeare: A Study of Facts and Problems* Oxford 1930 Volume II

64 http://shakespeare.mit.edu/

65 www.canadianshakespeares.ca

Appendix B

People

THE STORY WE have told in *On the Trail of the Real Macbeth* has involved a host of characters, many more than Shakespeare included in his famous play. An alphabetical list of the principal people mentioned in the book is included here together with a brief introduction to each. Their individual introduction to our story is noted in the Chapter and page number in brackets

Aed:
King of Alba from 877 to 878; son of Kenneth MacAlpin (Chapter 1, p. 31)

Banquo:
a fictional character used by Shakespeare in his play. Initially a friend to Macbeth, and supposedly an ancestor of the Stewart Kings of Scotland (Chapter 7, p. 125)

Bethoc:
daughter of Malcolm II; mother of Duncan I (Chapter 2, p. 41)

Boite:
son of Kenneth III; father of Gruoch (Chapter 2, p. 44)

Boite:
nephew of Gruoch; last direct male claimant for the kingship of Alba in the male line from Kenneth III (Chapter 3, p. 54)

Brendan the Navigator:
6th century Irish Christian missionary for whom Birnie Kirk was founded (Chapter 2, p. 47)

Bridei:	6th century ruler of the Northern Picts (Chapter 4, p. 80)
Crinan:	Abbot of Dunkeld; father of Duncan I and a rival of Macbeth (Chapter 2, p. 41)
Colum Cille:	known today as Columba, sixth century Christian missionary and founder of the famous monastery at Iona (Chapter 1, p. 25)
Conrad II:	elected King of Germany in 1024 and Holy Roman Emperor in 1027 (Chapter 1, p. 36)
Constantine I:	King of Alba from 863 to 877; son of Kenneth MacAlpin (Chapter 1, p. 31)
Canute:	King of England from 1016 to 1035, Denmark from 1018 to 1035 and Norway from 1028 to 1035 (Chapter 1, p. 36)
David I:	King of Scotland from 1124 to 1153 (Chapter 2, p. 49)
Doada:	daughter of Malcolm II; wife of Findláech and mother of Macbeth (Chapter 1, p. 32)
Donald III:	called Donald Ban, son of Duncan I; brother to Malcolm III and King of Alba from 1093 to 1094 (Chapter 4, p. 74)
Duncan I:	King of Alba from 1034 to 1040; son of Crinan (Chapter 3, p. 41) and believed to be 'Karl Hundasson' in the Orkneyinga saga (Chapter 3, p. 58)

Duff, or Dubh:	King of Alba from 962 to 967; according to one whom one legend was slain at Forres castle by the castellan who had been incited by his wife. The characters in this episode were changed in Shakepeare's play to Macbeth and Duncan (Chapter 7, p. 129)
Eadulf:	Earl of Northumbria (in Bernicia) from 1038 to 1041 (Chapter 3, p. 60)
Ealdgyth:	daughter of Uhtred, Earl of Northumbria; grand-daughter of Ethelred the Unready (Chapter 4, p. 74)
Echmarcach:	probable sub-King of Alba in the Western Isles, King of Dublin from 1036 to 1038 and from 1046 to 1052, and probably ruler in Man and Galloway in the latter period (Chapter 1, p. 36)
Edward the Confessor:	Anglo-Saxon King of England from 1042 to 1066 (Chapter 4, p. 74)
Edward 1:	King of England from 1239 to 1307 (Chapter 4, p. 69)
Ethelred the Unready:	Anglo-Saxon King of England from 978 to 1013 and from 1014 to 1016; father of Edward the Confessor (Chapter 4, p. 74)
Findláech:	father of Macbeth and Mormaer of Moray from before 1014 until 1020 (Chapter 1, p. 31)

Gilla Comgáin:	first cousin of Macbeth, Mormaer of Moray from 1029 until 1031. First husband of Gruoch and father of Lulach (Chapter 1, p. 29)
Godwin:	Earl of Wessex, father of Harold Godwinson (Harold II King of England); died 1053 (Chapter 6, p. 109)
Gospatric:	Earl of Northumbria from 1067 to 1068 and again from 1069 to 1072; son of Maldred, the brother of Duncan I King of Alba (Chapter 4, p. 76)
Gruoch:	wife of Macbeth; daughter of Boite, son of Kenneth III of Alba. Also wife of Gilla Comgáin and mother to Lulach (Chapter 2, p. 38)
Harold Godwinson:	King Harold II, last Anglo-Saxon King of England from January to October 1066 (Chapter 3, p. 62)
Harold Harefoot:	Son of Canute and King of England from 1035 to 1040 (Chapter 3, p. 60)
Harthacanute:	Son of Canute and King of Denmark from 1035 to 1040 and King of England from 1040 to 1042 (Chapter 3, p. 60)
Henry III:	son of Conrad II and crowned Holy Roman Emperor in 1046 (Chapter 5, p. 87)
Hugh:	A Norman who left England in 1053 for Alba with Osbern Pentecost (Chapter 6, p. 110)

Ingieborg: wife of Thorfinn, Earl of Orkney; then married Malcolm III of Alba (Chapter 6, p. 114)

Kenneth MacAlpin: King of Picts and Scots from 843 to 859 (Chapter 1, p. 31)

Kenneth III: King of Alba from 997 to 1005; grandfather of Gruoch (Chapter 2, p. 44)

Leo IX: Pope from 1049 to 1054 (Chapter 5, p. 87)

Lulach: Macbeth's stepson; son of Gruoch and Gilla Comgáin; King of Alba from 1057 to 1058 and known as 'Lulach the simple' or 'Lulach the fool' (Chapter 2, p. 45)

Macbeth: Macbethad mac Findláech, Mormaer of Moray and King of Alba from 1040 to 1057 (Chapter 1, p. 24)

MacDuff: Thane of Fife, a fictional character in Shakepeare's play hostile to Macbeth (Chapter 7, p. 124)

Máel Brigte: Macbeth's uncle; brother of Findláech and Mormaer of Moray before Findláech (Chapter 1, p. 29)

Malcolm mac Máel Brigte: first cousin of Macbeth and Mormaer of Moray from 1020 to 1029 (Chapter 1, p. 29)

Malcolm II: King of Alba from 1005 to 1034; son of Kenneth II and grandfather of Macbeth, Thorfinn and Duncan I (Chapter 1, p. 31)

Malcolm III

King of Alba from 1058 to 1093; son of Duncan I and named Canmore (Chapter 4, p. 74)

Maldred:

half brother to Duncan I; son of Crinan and married to the sister of Eadulf, Earl of Northumbria (Chapter 3, p. 54)

Marianus Scotus:

Irish monk and chronicler, died 1088 (Chapter 5, p. 86)

Muddan:

nephew to Duncan I; led an unsuccessful attack on Caithness in 1035 (Chapter 4, p. 56)

Osbern Pentecost:

Norman knight, fled England in 1053 and travelled to Alba to give service to Macbeth (Chapter 6, p. 110)

Owain:

King of Strathclyde, died at the battle of Carham in 1018 (Chapter 2, p. 43)

Ruadri:

father of Findláech; grandfather of Macbeth (Chapter 1, p. 29)

Serf:

early 6th century Scottish missionary from Fife (Chapter 6, p. 109)

Sigurd:

Earl of Orkney from 991 to 1014; father of Thorfinn (Chapter 1, p. 35)

Siward:

Earl of Northumbria from 1041 to 1055 (Chapter 4, p. 74)

Sweyn Forkbeard:

Father of Canute, died 1014 (Chapter 2, p. 42)

Thorfinn: grandson of Malcom II; ruler of
                              Caithness from 1014 and after-
                              wards Earl of Orkney; cousin to
                              Macbeth (Chapter 1, p. 35)

Uhtred: Earl of Northumbria from 1006
                              to 1016 (Chapter 2, p. 43)

Urban II: Pope from 1088 to 1099 (Chapter
                              5, p. 90)

William the Conqueror: Duke of Normandy and King of
                              England from 1066 to 1087
                              (Chapter 4, p. 76)

William the Lion: King of Scotland from 1165 to
                              1214 (Chapter 2, p. 47)

Appendix C

Chronology

THERE MAY BE uncertainty regarding some of the precise dates in Macbeth's life and times but the chronology presented here provides a good framework for understanding the real Macbeth.

c 900	The emergence of Alba as a discrete entity from the unification of the Picts and the Scots
1002	Birth of Duncan, son of Abbot Crinan of Dunkeld and Bethoc (daughter of Malcolm II)
c 1005	Birth of Macbeth, son of Findláech and Doada (daughter of Malcolm II)
	Malcolm II becomes King of Alba having killed his predecessor, Kenneth III
1006	Malcolm II defeated at Durham
1009	Birth of Thorfinn, son of Earl Sigurd of Orkney and an un-named daughter of Malcom II
1014	Battle of Clontarf where Earl Sigurd of Orkney dies and his son Thorfinn comes under the protection of King Malcolm II
1016	Canute becomes King of England, adding the kingdom of Denmark in 1018 and Norway and part of Sweden in 1028
1018	Battle of Carham. Lothian north of the Tweed ceded to the victorious Malcolm II by the defeated Northumbrians
1020	Macbeth's father Findláech killed by Macbeth's cousins, one of whom, Malcolm, became Mormaer of Moray in his place

1020	Macbeth flees to the court of King Malcolm II, although he may have been at court before this date
1029	Gilla Comgáin becomes Mormaer of Moray on the death of his brother Malcolm
1031	Canute invades Alba and forces the submission of Malcolm II and two other important leaders, one of whom was probably Macbeth
1032	Gilla Comgáin and his followers killed, presumably by Macbeth who succeeds him as Mormaer of Moray
1033	Macbeth marries Gilla Comgáin's widow, Gruoch
	Malcolm III orders the killing of Gruoch's nephew, a potential legitimate male claimant to the throne of Alba
1034	Death of Malcolm II
	Duncan becomes King of Alba
1035	Probable campaign by Duncan against the Vikings in the north
	Death of Canute
1038	Northumbrians ravage Cumbria, territory controlled by King Duncan
1040	Duncan leads an invasion of Northumbria and, like his grandfather, suffers defeat at Durham
	Duncan subsequently leads a force into Moray, perhaps to quell a rebellion by Macbeth, and is defeated and killed at Pitgaveny by Elgin
	Macbeth becomes King of Alba
1045	Abbot Crinan, Duncan's father, leads a rebellion against Macbeth and is killed in battle

1046   Northumbrians invade Alba. Macbeth seems to have suffered a reversal of fortune and lost part of the kingdom, possibly to Maldred, Duncan's brother, but recovered the lost territory when the Northumbians withdrew. There is some debate about the dating of the events of 1046 but our view is that the date as recorded is plausible

1050   Macbeth goes on pilgrimage to Rome. He may in practice have left Alba in 1049. It appears that Thorfinn of Orkney also went on pilgrimage to Rome at this time though we do not know whether they would have chosen to travel together

1053   Norman knights expelled from England given refuge in Alba

1054   Invasion of Alba by Malcolm, son of Duncan, accompanied by Northumbrian forces and some of King Edward the Confessor of England's Huscarles

       Macbeth defeated at Dunsinane and retreats northwards

1057   Macbeth defeated and killed by Malcolm

       Macbeth's stepson Lulach becomes King of Alba. Some historians suggest that he may have become King before this time, possibly ruling jointly with Macbeth, but we do not know this to be the case

1058   Lulach killed

       Malcolm becomes King of Alba and rules as Malcolm III

c 1360   John of Fordun publishes the *Chronicle of the Scottish People* characterising Macbeth as a murderer and tyrant c 1400   Andrew of Wyntoun writes his *Original Chronicle of Scotland* introducing three weird sisters to the Macbeth story

1527   Hector Boece publishes his *History of the Scottish People* introducing Banquo to the Macbeth story and describing Lady Macbeth as a power hungry queen

1564   William Shakespeare born in Stratford-upon-Avon, England

1577   Ralph Holinshed publishes the *Chronicles of England, Scotland and Ireland*, used as a key source by William Shakespeare

1599   William Shakespeare becomes joint proprietor of the Globe Theatre in London

1603   James VI of Scotland crowned James I of England

1605   The Gunpowder Plot when Guy Fawkes was caught attempting to blow up the Houses of Parliament in London

c 1606   William Shakespeare writes his *Tragedie of Macbeth* written for King James I of England

1611   First known performance of the *Tragedie of Macbeth*, with Richard Burbage in the title role

1623   The earliest surviving text of the *Tragedie of Macbeth* published in Shakespeare's First Folio

1642   English Puritans close down all theatres and places of entertainment and in 1644 pull down the Globe Theatre

1660   Professional acting resumed in Great Britain on the restoration of Charles II

1708   A novel, *The Secret History of Macbeth, King of Scotland*, is published by an anonymous author

1744	David Garrick's famous production of Macbeth opens in the Drury Lane theatre London
1847	Guiseppe Verdi finishes composing an opera in four parts, based on the life of Macbeth
1849	The New York Astor Place Riot takes place during a performance of Macbeth, killing 31 people
1916	Sir Herbert Beerbohm's silent film *Macbeth* released
1934	Charles Laughton stars as Macbeth at an Old Vic production that left out the opening scene with the three witches
1948	Orson Welles's film *Macbeth* released, based on an earlier 1936 'voodoo' *Macbeth* stage production
1955	Lawrence Olivier and Vivien Leigh star in *Macbeth* for a Stratford Shakespeare Memorial Theatre production
1971	Roman Polanski's film *Macbeth* released
1978	Nigel Tranter's novel *Macbeth the King* published
2007	Over 100,000 people attend Royal Shakespeare Company versions of *Macbeth* each year. This is a small number compared to the worldwide audience who continue to interact with William Shakespeare's play via the theatre, films, books and various other media channels. In summer 2007 the National Theatre of Scotland took Macbeth back to Moray with a special play *The Elgin Macbeth* staged in the ruins of Elgin Cathedral.

Appendix D

Selected Further Reading

THE SELECTION OF BOOKS listed here includes those books and articles we found especially useful in researching *On the Trail of the Real Macbeth*. The academic textbooks will lead you to more detailed references if required.

Aitchison, N. (2000)
Macbeth: Man and myth,
Stroud: Sutton Publishing.

   A good, readable account.

Bryant, C. (2008)
Macbeth: the graphic novel,
Litchborough: Classical Comics Ltd

   An innovative approach to making Shakespeare's Macbeth more accessible: available as original text, plain text and quick text versions of the play.

Burnett, A (2007)
Macbeth and all that,
Edinburgh, Birlinn

   An extremely entertaining history of Macbeth, written for children.

Cowan, E.J. (1993)
'The Historical Macbeth', pp. 117–141 in W.D.H. Sellar (ed.)
Moray Province and People
(Scottish Society for Northern Studies)

   An energetic study by one of Scotland's leading historians.

Driscoll, S. (2002)
Alba: the Gaelic Kingdom of Scotland AD *800–1124*,
Edinburgh, Birlinn.

> Clearly written and well illustrated account, produced in
> association with Historic Scotland

Woolf, A. (2007)
From Pictland to Alba 789–1070,
Edinburgh, Edinburgh University Press

> Lively, thought-provoking second volume of the excellent
> New Edinburgh History of Scotland

Appendix E

King Macbeth Touring Itinerary

Introduction

THE BEST WAY to explore the world of the real Macbeth is to travel through the actual landscapes in which the events of his life and times played out. This will give you an understanding of the all-important geographical dimension of the story and can take you to evocative places where your imagination will bring the history of 11th century Alba to life. There is no doubt that in order to understand history you need to touch it.

To help you, we have prepared a touring itinerary consisting of a number of day's activities. At the core of the itinerary is the story of Macbeth but we have also suggested some other things you can do on your journey.

The itinerary can be enjoyed in 'bite-sized' day-long excursions over a longer period or it can form the basis of an intensive seven-day (or longer) holiday. We have assumed that you will use a car as transport as you follow the trail of the real Macbeth, King of Alba. At times we will take you off the main tourist routes and public transport may be infrequent or unavailable so your journey on foot or by bicycle will be longer.

The itinerary starts and ends in Inverness, the capital city of the Highlands. Inverness has a good rail link from the south and a busy airport with a number of connections. There is a wide range of accommodation to suit your needs and budget and the best place for advice is the VisitScotland web site www.visitscotland.com or there is a Tourist Information Centre in the city centre (Castle Wynd, Inverness, 01463 234353)

The itinerary for each day describes the recommended route and the locations to visit. We have tried to echo the chronology of Macbeth's story in the progression of the itinerary but this has not always been possible as we want to avoid the need for you to retrace your footsteps too far or too much.

We have included addresses, principal location references to the maps in this book, phone numbers, post codes and/or web site addresses in the itineraries to help you plan your own personal journey.

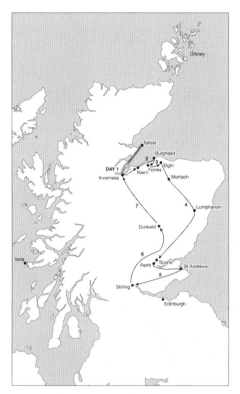

Figure 4: Overview of the itinerary

Please respect the natural and built environment as you follow this itinerary. Note that the information in the itinerary is accurate to the best of our knowledge at the time of writing but neither the authors nor the publisher can take responsibility for errors or omissions.

Day 1

WE'D LIKE YOU to start your Macbeth journey in the village of Dores (A1) (www.doresonlochness.co.uk), just less than nine miles south of Inverness on the B862. The road is a quiet one compared to the busier A82 on the other side of Loch Ness and it continues southwards to Fort Augustus. Park near the loch and you can enjoy spectacular views looking southwards along the length of Loch Ness. Here you are probably on the southern edge of the Province of Moray, in which Macbeth was born around 1005. Here, too, away from the small bustling city of Inverness, you get a sense of the drama of the landscape and it is easy to imagine Macbeth in this place as a young man.

Now retrace your route back into the centre of Inverness. The best place to get an overview of the history of Inverness and the wider region – from the rocks beneath your feet to life in the Highlands today – is Inverness Museum and Art Gallery (A3). The museum is open from 10:00 to 17:00 Monday to Saturday and admission is free. None of the items currently on display has a direct connection with Macbeth but the collection is an interesting one. The view of the town centre from the window in the medieval gallery is a good reminder that, despite the preponderance of modern buildings, Inverness has medieval and earlier origins. Inverness Museum can be found at Castle Wynd, Inverness, IV2 3EB (http://inverness.highland.museum).

Note that the Inverness Tourist Information Centre is just round the corner from the museum so now would be a good time to stock up on leaflets, brochures and travel and accommodation information.

As you exit the museum you will see a hill immediately in front of you. This is Castle Hill and you can take the short walk to the summit if you wish. The building that tops the hill was built in the 19th century and houses the County Hall. There was a series of earlier castles on the site dating back to the reign of Malcolm III (Malcolm Canmore) who built the first earth and timber enclosure here. From the top of the hill you get a good sense of the strategic importance of the site.

As we saw in Macbeth's story, it was Malcolm III who defeated and killed Macbeth to take the throne of Alba in his place. Malcolm's choice of Castle Hill as the location for a new fortress is significant because Macbeth's fortress was elsewhere in Inverness. It is believed to lie in the vicinity of Auldcastle Road (A4) in the area of the city known, tellingly, as The Crown. Though you can reach there by car – it is a peaceful, pleasant residential street – you can get a more dramatic idea of the location by parking in the supermarket car park beside Inverness railway station, crossing the main road (Millburn Road) and taking the footpath up the hill to Auldcastle Road. You will arrive breathless and in no position to challenge the hilltop's defenders.

The view from Auldcastle Road out across the Moray Firth is extensive and it is easy to appreciate why this spot had been a fortified place from the earliest times. Few of the train passengers coming and going from Inverness Station will realise that they are being watched by the ghosts of lookouts long dead. There has been some limited archaeological investigation of the area around Auldcastle Road and the results, intriguingly, really do suggest that there was an early fortification here and we believe this to be the location of Macbeth's castle in Inverness. There are no interpretation boards or leaflets available here so you are left with your imagination, but just stand by the side of the road and look out over Macbeth's domain. At this point in our story, however, bear in mind that this was not yet Macbeth's domain. His father Findláech was the Mormaer of Moray and controlled the fortress at Auldcastle Road. It was to be some years – years of exile – before Macbeth was able to claim his right to rule Moray.

In our account of the real Macbeth's early years we envisage him fleeing north on hearing the news of the murder of his father. To follow him, return to your car and head north on the A9 across the Kessock Bridge on the outskirts of the city. You have entered a region known as the Black Isle and of course Macbeth would have made the short journey by boat.

The Black Isle is rich agricultural land and was extensively settled by Pictish peoples in earlier centuries. In the early 11th century the

Vikings and Scots competed for control of land and the region would have been a dangerous place to be if you lacked the means to defend yourself. It has a more peaceful character today and many people commute from here into the growing city of Inverness to work.

Continue north along the A9 for another four and a half miles or so until you reach the Tore roundabout. Here, take the exit for the A832 and head east towards the town of Cromarty via Fortrose and Rosemarkie (A5) (www.fortrosemarkie.org). The cathedral ruins in Fortrose are all that remain of a beautiful building built in 1250. Nearby Chanonry Point is a great place to get a view of a more intimidating piece of architecture: Fort George across the Moray Firth. The Fort was built in the 18th century following the defeat of the Jacobite rebels at nearby Culloden and it is still a working garrison.

You may be lucky and see some more peaceful neighbours, however, as Chanonry Point is well known as a viewing spot for the community of dolphins that live in the Moray Firth.

A little further east is Rosemarkie, famous for its Pictish carved stones now housed in the Groam House Museum, High Street, Rosemarkie IV10 8UF (www.groamhouse.org.uk). Even though there is no connection with Macbeth the Museum is well worth visiting. Opening times vary through the year so check the web site in advance. Rosemarkie is an ancient religious centre, St Boniface's shrine having long been a place of pilgrimage.

Continue along the road through the Black Isle until you reach the beautifully preserved 18th century town of Cromarty (A6) (www.black-isle.info/Cromarty), from where you can enjoy superb views of the Moray Firth. The Firth was a highway for 11th century travellers who would have made journeys by boat whereas modern travellers tend to travel by car. In the summer months you can get the best of both worlds and take the Cromarty-Nigg ferry across to the Tarbat peninsula to the north. This avoids the need to drive back west to the Tore roundabout to rejoin the A9 and will give you a short taste of the sea on board this tiny two-car ferry.

If you have time, Cromarty Courthouse Museum (www.cromarty-courthouse.org.uk) is an interesting place to visit even though it deals with times long after Macbeth's day.

Once across the ferry follow the signs leading you about 10 miles north east towards Portmahomack. This pretty seaside village is in an idyllic location and it is an ancient settlement. As you arrive in the village look out for signs to your right directing you to the Tarbat Discovery Centre (A7). It is located in an attractive former church on the outskirts of the village and there is ample car parking. The bronze statue of a Pictish Princess that you will see beside the church wall is a clue that you have arrived at a special place, indeed.

The Tarbat Discovery Centre, Tarbatness Road, Portmahomack IV20 1YA (www.tarbat-discovery.co.uk) tells the story of the Pictish monastic settlement that has been excavated nearby over a period of years. The excavations have been completed for the moment but the Discovery Centre brings the story to life. A church existed here as early as the 8th century and it remained an important religious centre in Macbeth's day. He would have known of this place and if, as we suggest in telling his story, he fled from Inverness northwards it is possible that he stopped to pray here and to ask for help from the monks.

Return to your car and continue along the road past the Discovery Centre towards Tarbat Ness lighthouse (A8). The car park is well signposted. The lighthouse, established in 1830, was engineered by Robert Stevenson but we have brought you to this spot for two reasons connected with Macbeth. Firstly, in our re-telling of Macbeth's flight following the murder of his father we speculate on his thoughts as he stands looking southwards from where you stand now.

The second reason – and here we need to jump forwards in our story – is that King Duncan of Alba fought a battle at Tarbat Ness against Earl Thorfinn of Orkney. Just imagine standing here watching the ships approach each other slowly, the preparations for battle clear enough to see and the noise increasing as battle is joined. As you stand at Tarbat Ness you may, indeed, have more modern warriors for company, albeit briefly: aircraft of the RAF are regular visitors here as they fly in from the sea towards a bombing range near the town of Tain to the west of you.

To end this first day of your itinerary, drive back past the Tarbat Discovery Centre and leave Portmahomack behind you, travelling south west via the village of Fearn to join the main A9. Head south to Inverness, then 16 miles east on the A96 to the small town of Nairn. This is an ideal place to stay ready to continue your journey of exploration tomorrow.

Day Two

Suitably rested after a busy first day, we hope that you are ready to continue your journey. Today you will travel eastwards into Moray, closer to the heart of Macbeth's story.

But as in every good story you need to go back in order to go forwards so we'd like you to join the main A96 and head westwards towards Inverness for just over five miles before turning left at the B9006. Then, after less than half a mile, take the B9090 – which follows the route of an old military road – south east towards Cawdor Castle (www.cawdorcastle.co.uk). Shakespeare's play made Cawdor famous and forever associated it in popular imagination with Macbeth, so-called Thane of Cawdor. But Cawdor Castle was not built until the 14th century so there can be no connection with the real Macbeth.

The castle is a beautiful, fascinating place with magnificent gardens and is well worth visiting for its own sake and because of the Shakespearean connection. It is privately owned, has a range of visitor facilities and is open from May to October, seven days a week. Take time, too, to wander through Cawdor village itself.

Your next destination is the village of Auldearn (B1), just six miles to the east. When you are ready to depart Cawdor, rejoin the B9090 and drive east, continuing along the B9101 to Auldearn. Follow the signs for the Boath Doocot, a nicely restored dovecote set on top of a much earlier castle motte or mound. The motte is all that remains of a castle built there in the reign of William the lion in about 1180. There is a small car park at the base of the motte and a path leads to the top.

The view from the top is excellent and in our story about the real Macbeth we speculate that this may perhaps have been the location of the burning of Gilla Comgáin and his band in a fortified house. Imagine standing here with Macbeth as he looks at the smoking remains of the house and contemplates his future.

While you are here, also, read the interpretation panel on top of the motte. It explains the events of 1645 when, at the Battle of Auldearn, the Marquis of Montrose defeated a numerically superior army of Covenanters. Another notable episode in Scotland's eventful, turbulent history, 600 years after Macbeth's time.

Return to your car and drive through the village of Auldearn then rejoin the A96, going right to continue your journey eastwards. Travel the four miles to the village of Brodie and go left, signposted for Brodie Castle. Just over the level crossing, look out for a signpost directing you north then west to Macbeth's Hillock. There is space to pull off the road beside a wooden fingerpost sign, leading you through a field to a large mound. This is Macbeth's Hillock, where local folklore claims that Macbeth and Banquo had their first encounter with the three witches. The view north from the hillock is a good one, and bear in mind that the coastline may have been a little closer in Macbeth's time and the land a bit marshier. The hillock is a good place to reflect on Macbeth's story; even though you can see the main A96 nearby there is a strong sense of place here. Folklore, of course, can mislead us and the reality is that there are no contemporary records of Macbeth meeting witches here or anywhere else, and Banquo had no historical existence whatsoever.

Assuming you are not waylaid by witches, return to your car. Continue in the direction your car is facing and you will shortly rejoin the A96. Go left and make the short journey to Brodie village again. Brodie Countryfare (www.brodiecountryfare.com) is open seven days a week and offers high quality shopping as well as an excellent restaurant.

Nearby Brodie Castle (www.nts.org.uk) is a 16th century tower house and gardens in the care of the National Trust for Scotland. It is open from March to October. There is a Pictish symbol stone in the grounds of the castle, originally found in nearby Dyke village churchyard. This is the only visible evidence of the earliest settlement of the area but we can be fairly sure that there would have been farms here in the early 11th century if the Picts thought the place important enough to place a stone here hundreds of years earlier.

Now rejoin the A96 and continue to make your way eastwards. You are going to the ancient Pictish fortress of Burghead (C2). The town of Forres is about four miles away. Go straight ahead at the first roundabout then at the second roundabout take the first exit signposted for the B9011 to Kinloss. When you reach Kinloss go straight ahead at the traffic lights on to the B9089. Follow this for six and a half miles all the way to Burghead and drive through the town's grid-like pattern of streets towards the headland beside the sea.

Burghead was an important Pictish fortress and port from around 300 to 800, when it was attacked and destroyed by Vikings. The site would have remained of strategic importance thereafter and when presumed Viking occupation was finally driven out by the Scots, perhaps at the start of the 11th century, it would be surprising if the Mormaers of Moray did not make use of the site as part of the chain of fortified residences across the Province.

Sadly, as you will see when you arrive in Burghead, the orderly minds of Victorian industrialists imposed an order on the town that erased much of the Pictish fort but there is still enough there to impress. Having parked your car, walk to the whitewashed building, formerly a Coastguard lookout. The view from the top of the building is magnificent and there are interpretation panels that help make sense of what you see. The Burghead Headland Trust (www.burghead.com) operates a visitor centre inside the Coastguard lookout between April and September and this is a good way to enhance your understanding of the site. The Burghead fort is famous for its bull carvings and two of these can be seen in the visitor centre.

Look out for the signposts to Burghead Well in King Street.

This is a rock-cut well identified by some as an early Christian shrine associated with St Ethan. The well is in the care of Historic Scotland (www.historic-scotland.gov.uk) and the key to the site – which is kept locked to prevent misuse – is available locally. It is an evocative place to visit and shouldn't be missed.

Higher sea levels in Macbeth's time meant that Burghead was virtually an island and it would have been a highly defensible position, as well as having an important symbolic importance both because of its long, proud, Pictish past but also its recent occupation by Vikings from the north. Before you leave the headland, look back across the town, and down over the harbour built by Thomas Telford, and try to imagine what it must have been like in Macbeth's time. Almost certainly there were buildings, and probably also a church. Beyond, inland, was the fertile plain of Moray and beyond that the hills became mountains, protecting the Province from the south. If Macbeth stood here and looked in the direction you are now looking he would have felt satisfaction at the agricultural richness of this part of his domain.

Retrace your route now, leaving Burghead on the B9089 and travelling west to Kinloss. Kinloss is an important RAF base and you may have airborne warriors for company as you drive. When you arrive in Kinloss, just after the fence around the base and just before the traffic lights, take the track to the left signposted to Kinloss Abbey (www.kinlossabbey.co.uk). The Abbey, little of which remains standing in the small churchyard, was established by King David I in 1150 and stood on the probable route from the port of Findhorn to the town of Forres. The foundation of the Abbey, and its location, was part of David I's attempt to control the independent-minded Province of Moray more than 100 years after Macbeth's death.

Kinloss Abbey stands as an example of how places can change over time. Today, the site is easily missed and often bypassed by visitors but in its time it was an important centre of learning and represented a considerable investment of Royal energy and resources. There is a connection, too, with one of the locations you visited on the first day of your itinerary: having been abandoned in the Reformation of 1560 the Abbey's stonework was sold to Oliver Cromwell in 1650 and used in the construction of Inverness Castle.

Leave the Abbey and follow the B9011 back to Forres where you will stay overnight. Tomorrow is a momentous day in Macbeth's story.

Day Three

If your overnight accommodation was near the town centre and if the weather is fine you may prefer to explore Forres on foot.

Forres (www.forres-net.co.uk) is an ancient town, despite its rather Victorian appearance. Walk down the High Street and you may sense the medieval origins of the town, with small lanes running off a central road. Take some time this morning to explore the Falconer Museum (www.falconermuseum.co.uk) near the Market Cross and Tolbooth in the centre of the High Street. The museum was established in the 19th century and has recently been refurbished. The Forres Tourist Information Centre is located in the same building so use the opportunity to gather local information leaflets. The Museum and information centre are open seasonally and you should check details on the Falconer Museum web site before visiting.

If you have not already picked one up elsewhere, look for a King Macbeth leaflet in the information centre. The leaflet, which can also be downloaded from www.kingmacbeth.com, accompanies an audio tour that you can dial up and listen to as you follow Macbeth's tale today. At three locations – Sueno's Stone (Forres), Pitgaveney (near Elgin) and Elgin Museum – Macbeth tells his own dramatic story.

Leaving the museum, turn left and walk to the west end of the High Street. The small park here at Castlehill was the site of a Royal castle from the 12th century onwards when the town became a Royal Burgh. But there was an earlier fortification nearby. Walk back along the High Street and Victoria Road until you come to Grant Park. You'll know it by the award-winning floral sculptures in this attractive public park. Sheltering the park is a large hill, known as

Cluny Hill (c1). Follow one of the paths to the top of the hill, looking out for fingerposts directing you to Nelson Tower. This impressive white tower was built in 1806 to commemorate Admiral Lord Nelson's victory at the Battle of Trafalgar. It is managed by Moray Council's Museums Service and is open to the public most afternoons between May and September. Check opening times at the Falconer Museum.

The view over the surrounding landscape from the top of the tower is a commanding one and we believe that there would have been an important fortification here in Macbeth's time, possibly one of his principal residences. Standing at this point it is easy to imagine Macbeth and Gruoch here too, looking out over their lands. In our story about Macbeth's life we suggest that the couple were indeed here on one momentous day in August 1040, the day on which Macbeth confronted and killed King Duncan.

Walk back down the hill and through Grant Park to Victoria Road. Continue walking east away from the town centre and look out for the large rounded stone beside the pavement near the Police Station. As the small plaque explains, the stone is believed to be of Pictish origin and marks the site where in later times witches were said to have been rolled down Cluny Hill in barrels. Not, we are sure, voluntarily.

Now cross to the other side of Victoria Road and continue east about 300 yards before turning down Findhorn Road, a quiet side street. Note the signpost directing you to Sueno's Stone (c3) just a few more yards down the road. Tucked down this residential street is a truly astounding monument – a 23 feet tall Pictish carved stone. The stone, in the care of Historic Scotland (www.historic-scotland.gov.uk) and protected from the elements by a glass enclosure, dates to the 9th or 10th centuries so would have stood on this spot in Macbeth's time. He, too, must have stood beside the stone and marvelled at it. One side of the stone has a Christian cross while the other side has a series of carvings, now quite badly eroded. These tell a story of some kind though interpretations differ as to the story being told. Perhaps most likely is that the stone was erected by Kenneth MacAlpin to commemorate a victory over the Picts; the stone would therefore have been erected to celebrate his victory but also to remind his enemies of his power and prestige.

There is a local legend – probably dating only as far back as Shakespeare's time – that the three witches Macbeth encountered are trapped inside the stone and will escape if the stone ever breaks.

There is no charge for access to Sueno's Stone and there is a small car park beside it. Don't forget to listen to the first part of the Macbeth audio story here; in it, Macbeth stands beside this monument reflecting on his rightful ambition to be King of Alba.

When you are ready, it is time to return to your car and rejoin the A96 to travel eastwards once more, heading for Spynie Palace (C4) near Elgin. Continue along the A96 for about nine and a half miles until you reach the outskirts of Elgin. At the speed limit signs just beside the Eight Acres Hotel, turn left onto Morriston Road. Drive all the way along this road (1.2 miles) then go left on to the A941/North Street and continue for a mile and a half until you reach the signpost directing you right to Spynie Palace. There is a car park at the end of the access road.

This area is called Pitgaveney and is believed to be the location of Macbeth's confrontation with King Duncan. The landscape has changed a great deal here. The car park was on the shoreline of a Loch in Macbeth's day and the loch enabled ships to sail in and beach here. Look north from the car park and you will note how the land shelves steeply: where there are trees now there was once the sea.

Arriving here Macbeth would have been aware of the invading force led by Duncan. Listen to the second part of the audio story to hear Macbeth's thoughts at this time.

Spynie Palace itself is a fascinating place to visit, though there are no remains from the 11th century here. The palace was the residence of the Bishops of Moray for 500 years until 1686 and the remains are now in the care of Historic Scotland (www.historic-scotland.gov.uk) whose web site gives details of opening times and admission charges. There is an excellent selection of books in the small shop run by Historic Scotland.

When you are ready, leave Spynie Palace, going left on to the road back to Elgin. Follow the A941/North Street all the way into town then take the first exit at the roundabout on to the A96. After about 350 yards, turn left into North College Street and park your car. You have arrived at Elgin Cathedral (C5).

Elgin Cathedral, King St, Elgin, IV30 1HU, the so-called Lantern of the North, has been described as one of Scotland's most beautiful medieval buildings. The first church on this site dates back to the 1200s, long after Macbeth's death, but in the third part of the audio story this is the location to which the wounded King Duncan was brought, and where he died from his wounds thus clearing the way for Macbeth to lay claim to the throne of Alba.

Elgin Cathedral is cared for by Historic Scotland (www.historic-scotland.gov.uk). Don't miss the octagonal Chapter House and, so long as you don't mind heights, climb to the top of the cathedral tower and enjoy the view. Highly recommended, but only in fine weather.

Elgin Museum, 1 High St, Elgin, IV30 1EQ (www.elginmuseum. org.uk) was founded in 1836, making it possibly the oldest independent museum in Scotland. It is a short walk away from the Cathedral. The museum is a first class introduction to Moray and its people and there is information available regarding Macbeth including a display giving a timeline of his life – a useful reminder as you follow his story.

There is one more place – a very special place – to visit today: Birnie Kirk (B2). Return to your car and drive down North College Street with Elgin Cathedral on your left. At the end of the road, turn right into Pansport Road and when you reach the roundabout take the second exit and follow Maisondieu Road for about half a mile. Then, at the roundabout, take the first exit on to the A941/New Elgin Road and continue along this road for about three miles, crossing two roundabouts en route. You will then see a signpost directing you right, towards Birnie no more than a mile and half away. There is a small car park beside the churchyard.

You will feel the atmosphere of this place the moment you step out of your car. It feels ancient and peaceful, far from the hustle and bustle of our modern world. The site is indeed an ancient one as the Pictish stone in the churchyard testifies. The circular and walled churchyard is on a raised mound and the earliest church here was dedicated to St Brendan the Navigator. This is truly a Celtic Christian site. The church building you see today was built around 1140, replacing an earlier church, and is still in use having been modified over the centuries. The Kirk had an illustrious past, being the first cathedral of the Bishopric of Moray

The church building is open at most times. Perhaps the greatest treasure inside the church is the rectangular Coronach Bell, a Celtic bell that is about 1,000 years old making it contemporary with Macbeth. In the story we tell of Macbeth and Gruoch we speculate on the possibility that the couple may have married in Birnie Kirk and, therefore, the bell may have been rung to celebrate the occasion. An intriguing possibility and a real connection with the past.

When you have explored the church and churchyard, retrace your route and return to Elgin where you will stay tonight, a chance to relax and reflect on a busy day behind you.

Day Four

On this fourth day of your itinerary we will, because of the logic of travel rather than the flow of the narrative, have to move backwards and forwards through Macbeth's story.

You may remember driving south from Elgin along the A941/ New Elgin Road on the way to Birnie yesterday. Today, drive along the same road but ignore the Birnie turn-off and continue down the A941 to Dufftown about 17 miles away. As you'll notice from the number of distilleries in the vicinity of the town, Dufftown has legitimate claim to the title of malt whisky capital of the world and you may wish to give in to temptation and visit one of the distilleries. The Glenfiddich distillery (http://uk. glenfiddich. com/distillery/ index.html) is perhaps the best known and a visit to the award-winning distillery visitor centre would be time well spent.

Dufftown as you see it is a 19th century planned town but it has much older origins and was originally called Mortlach. Mortlach

Parish Church (B3) is one of the oldest places of Christian worship in Scotland, founded in 566 by St Moluag. To find it, when you arrive in the centre of Dufftown and the A941 takes a sharp left turn, go straight ahead instead, following Church Street to the bottom of the hill where you can park safely and then walk into Mortlach church-yard. This is a peaceful, evocative place and it is easy to see why early Christians chose to settle here. Just like Birnie there is a Pictish carved stone to demonstrate the importance of the site. Mortlach was an established Celtic Christian settlement in Macbeth's day.

We believe that Macbeth would have had a fortified residence in Mortlach or perhaps on one of the nearby hills and it is likely that he would have used some of the monastic community as administrators in his household, as well as their religious duties. Mortlach has a strategic location as a north-south gateway.

There is a pleasant, atmospheric riverside walk along the river Dullen near Mortlach church. Look out for the fingerposts directing you to the Giant's Chair, a natural seat in the rocks beside a deep pool. It is easy to imagine 11th century war bands moving quietly along the path, balancing haste with stealth. There are accounts, indeed, of conflict between Vikings and Scots near Mortlach so such speculation may not be too far off the mark.

Having avoided being caught up in any Viking raids, return to your car and drive back along Church Street, rejoining the A941 southwards. Your destination this time is Mossat, just 21 miles away. Stay on the A941 for about 12½ miles and then turn right at the B9002. Stay on the B9002 for just over four and half miles and then go right at the A97. Stay on the A97 for some three and a half miles until you reach the Mossat turn-off and park in the small car park next to the fish farm. As you drove down from Dufftown did you get the sense of the landscape changing? The hills and mountains of the north were very real barriers in Macbeth's time and you can still get a sense of this by imagining what it would be like to travel on foot or on horseback. This is what made Dufftown (Mortlach) so strategically important as a gateway.

We have brought you to an area called Essie in the region formerly called Strathbogie. Jumping ahead in Macbeth's story, this is the vicinity where Macbeth's stepson Lulach met his death in 1058. We don't know exactly where and, in fact, there are several Pictish or earlier standing stones that later became known as Lulach's Stone, with folklore claiming that this or the other was the place of the young and unfortunate King's death. Of course the reality is that we don't know which stone, if any, it really was but there is a standing stone on the hillside to your south west that may be the place. The site itself is hidden amongst trees and access is difficult and muddy so we do not recommend attempting to reach it. But just look around you and imagine what it must have been for Lulach to meet his death near here, outside his Moray homeland.

Now drive on, heading down the A944 signposted for Alford. After just over six miles, take the A980 south the 10½ miles to Lumphanan (E8). When you get to the village, drive through it until you go past Macbeth's Tavern (a rather appropriate place for coffee or lunch!) then go right at the junction and follow the signs for the Peel Ring of Lumphanan. There is a car park here.

Lumphanan is the place where, in 1057, King Macbeth was defeated and killed by Malcolm Canmore as the King retreated northwards to Moray following his defeat at Dunsinane. Legend has it that Macbeth stopped here to rest and get water from a well – now known as Macbeth's Well – but was brought to battle and killed. The local story continues that he was beheaded at a stone now called Macbeth's Stone and his headless body buried at Macbeth's Cairn to the north of the village before being taken to Iona for proper burial. We cannot tell the truth of these local stories but they paint an evocative picture of the last hours and minutes of Macbeth.

The Peel Ring of Lumphanan is a much later structure, the remains of an impressive motte and bailey castle dating to the 12th century. Though it has no connection with Macbeth it is an excellent place to stand and view the surrounding landscape, and to reflect on Macbeth's life – and death – at this place.

We have jumped to the end of the story here, however, and there is still much to see and do. Return to your car and leave the Peel Ring car park, turning right to drive eastwards on the A980 past

Lumphanan village. Continue along the A980 to Banchory, some 10 miles or so away. There, take the A93 westwards and look out for the B974 on your left. Join the B974 and follow it southwards over the mountains. The highest point you reach is Cairn o'Mount (E6), about 1,490 feet above sea level. There is a viewpoint here and you should stop to take in the view southwards. For Macbeth and his followers this panorama of the agricultural riches of Alba must have been a thrilling sight.

Continue southwards until the B974 meets the A90, then turn right to travel south. After about 18¼ miles, take the A94 west towards Glamis (E5). Macbeth never was Thane of Glamis as Shakespeare asserts; in fact there is no documented association between Macbeth and Glamis at all but it is a fascinating place to visit all the same.

Glamis Castle, Glamis, Angus, DD8 1RJ (www.glamis-castle.co.uk) was the childhood home of the late Queen Elizabeth the Queen Mother and it is a beautiful building surrounded by attractive gardens. It is open from March to December but check the web site for information about the range of visitor facilities before you visit.

There is an ancient stone in the nearby village said to be a monument to Malcolm II who died there in 1034. There is some evidence that Malcolm died trying to quell unrest in Moray, so perhaps the connection between Macbeth's story and Glamis is not just a figment of Shakespeare's imagination.

When you are ready, return to your car and continue south west along the A94 to Scone or perhaps a little further onwards to Perth if you prefer, to stay overnight.

As you relax this evening, think of how Macbeth must have felt the evening before his own visit to Scone. Tomorrow he will become King of Alba, King of the Scots.

Day Five

You might have been surprised when you reached Scone yesterday to discover that there are actually two Scones: Old Scone and New Scone. The medieval settlement at Scone, which included a monastery and royal residence, was abandoned in the 19th century when the population was moved to New Scone (now referred to simply as Scone) in order to make way for the local landowner, the Earl of Mansefield, to build a new palace. It is strange to think that the historic capital of Alba – the inauguration place of the Kings of Alba – was swept away in the name of progress, albeit it was replaced by a building, Scone Palace, whose architecture and gardens are beautiful in their own right. Scone Palace, Perth, PH2 6BD (www.scone-palace.net) is the home of the Earl and Countess of Mansefield but is open to visitors between March and October. Check the web site for details. There is ample car parking, a restaurant and shop amongst a range of facilities.

During your visit to Scone Palace, make your way to the Moot Hill (D1). This is the place where Kings of Alba were inaugurated, seated or standing on the Stone of Destiny in sight of their followers, clergymen, including those from Scone's Culdee community, and the principal leaders of the kingdom. Imagine this place without the more modern buildings around it. You are with Macbeth as he steps forward, embracing his own destiny as he mounts the Stone of Destiny. Perhaps there was an initial hush, a collective holding of breath as the religious rites began; and then a roar of acclamation as the new King of Alba looked proudly down on the assembled multitude.

The original Stone of Destiny is now in Edinburgh Castle, having been returned to Scotland after its centuries of exile in London. The stone you see on Moot Hill is a replica, but this is an evocative place to stand when you visit this place, so important in the history of Scotland.

Macbeth would have stayed in Scone immediately after his inauguration, celebrating success, cementing relationships, making plans and settling the details of his personal rule. You, however, need to continue with your own journey.

It is about 23 miles from Old Scone to Dundee. Head south on the A93 towards Perth, then after about a mile and a half look out for signs for the A85 continuing southwards for a further mile and a half before joining the A90. Once on the A90 you will see the Firth of Tay on your right. The sea was an important highway for travellers in Macbeth's time and we assume that he would have travelled from Elgin to Scone by sea, following the coastline all the way down. Your road journey, however, will take you via Dundee to the historic University town of St Andrews, the home of golf but also more importantly the ecclesiastical centre of Scotland from the 10th century when it took over that role from Dunkeld.

Continue along the A90 for 15½ miles until you come to a round-about on the outskirts of the city of Dundee. There, take the third exit, signposted for the A85/Riverside Avenue and carry along this road for four miles then follow the signs for the A92 across the Tay Bridge. Follow the A92 for about three miles then at the Forgan Roundabout take the first exit on to the A914, which you should follow for almost three miles before joining the A919. After a further two and three quarter miles, take the first exit at the roundabout on to the A91 towards St Andrews about four miles away. Once in the town, follow local signage for St Andrew's Cathedral and St Rule's Tower.

This has been a Christian site since around 732 when the relics of St Andrew were brought here. The remains of St Andrew's Cathedral and St Rule's Tower are in the care of Historic Scotland (www.historic-scotland.gov.uk) and there is a museum and shop on site. The cathedral, which post-dates Macbeth's time, was once Scotland's largest church and the remains are impressive. St Rule's Tower was part of an earlier building, some of which dates to the 11th century. The tower is over 100 feet high and the view from the top – if you have a head for heights – is spectacular. Check the Historic Scotland web site for details of opening times and prices and, if you have time, visit the nearby castle too. For general information about St Andrews have a look at www.standrews.co.uk.

Macbeth would undoubtedly have visited St Andrews during his kingship of Alba if not before when he was in Malcolm II's household.

His reasons for doing so would have been both political and spiritual. If, as some people think, Gruoch came from Fife or had family connections to the area, she too would have been well acquainted with the monastic community of St Andrews. There is more direct evidence for Macbeth and Gruoch's relationship with the church further east, at Loch Leven (D3), where they gave grants of land to a Culdee community. Loch Leven, then, is your next destination.

Leave St Andrews southwards on the A915, driving for 16 miles until the Durievale roundabout where you should take the second exit on to the A911. Stay on this road for 11 miles, passing Glenrothes en route, and then go left on to the B920 for a mile and three quarters before turning right on to the B9097. Loch Leven is on your right hand side. A mile down this road the Vane Farm RSPB centre (RSPB Vane Farm Nature Reserve, by Loch Leven. Kinross, KY13 9LX (www.rspb.org.uk), part of the Loch Leven National Nature Reserve, has visitor facilities including a café, interpretive materials and a shop and you should park here and visit the centre.

There are good views over Loch Leven to the small island of St Serfs where there was a Culdee community in Macbeth's time; this was the community Macbeth and Gruoch's grants of lands was intended to support. The island is a bird sanctuary and is not readily accessible.

There is another island on Loch Leven which is accessible in the summer months, however, and it is well worth visiting. Continue west along the B9097 and after about two miles go north on the B996 to Kinross a further two and a half miles away. The B996 runs parallel to the M90 motorway and gives good views of Loch Leven on your right. When you get to Kinross, follow local signage to the car park on the west shore of the Loch. Here, from April to September, a small ferry operated by Historic Scotland will take you to Loch Leven Castle (www.historic-scotland.gov.uk), a romantic ruin on an island in the loch. The castle, which dates back to the late 14th century, is perhaps most famous as the place where Mary Queen of Scots was imprisoned and forced to abdicate. Impressive as it is, the castle was not completely secure; the doomed Queen escaped from the castle.

When you have made your own escape from the castle, return to your car and follow local signage in Kinross for the A977 going west. After three quarters of a mile go right, following the B918 for less than a mile and a half before it joins the A91 heading west to Stirling about 20 miles away. Stirling has played a crucial part in Scotland's history, though the connection with Macbeth is not an especially strong one. But no itinerary through the heart of the Scotland can ignore William Wallace, Robert the Bruce and the Battle of Bannockburn and we'd like you to stay overnight in Stirling to take in some of the atmosphere of this fascinating place. Tomorrow you will have an opportunity to explore it for yourself, a day off from our *Macbethean* journey!

Day Six

Today we'd like to depart from our usual detailed itinerary and instead offer you the opportunity to explore Stirling and this historic area in your own way and at your own pace. Today, then, you step out of the Macbeth story and experience some other aspects of Scotland's history. Of course, if you are short of time, today's itinerary can be omitted from your plans altogether.

We have several suggestions of places to visit today. Stirling Castle, dominating the town and surrounding landscape from its commanding position, is an iconic site and should not be missed. In the past the surrounding landscape was much wetter and marshier than today, making Stirling and its castle of enormous strategic significance in central Scotland. Stirling Castle is in the care of Historic Scotland (www.historic-scotland.gov.uk) and is open all year, seven days a week. Check the web site for opening times and details of visitor facilities.

The views from the battlements of Stirling Castle are rivalled by those from the Wallace Monument, located just outside Stirling. The monument to Scotland's national hero (www.nationalwallace monument.com) is open daily all year and, as usual, you should check the web site for opening times and other information.

Standing on top of the Wallace Monument you are briefly back in Macbeth's story. We said in Chapter seven that he may have watched Norman knights entering the heartland of Alba from close by. To the south, you can trace the old route across the marshes the knights would have taken, across the Causewayhead. To the north-west lie the ruins of Logie Church (E1), where we suggested that Macbeth may have waited for them. You can spot this church by looking across the modern University, nestled in the hill beyond, just past the small golf course.

Staying with Macbeth for just a short while, when you leave the Wallace Monument take a short drive into the centre of Bridge of Allan, just past the University. This picturesque spa town has some delightful shops and cafes, and at the end of the main street lays a small bridge across the River Allan. This is the start of the Darn walkway (E2) where Macbeth's party would have passed by to reach Dunblane to the north-west.

We will re-connect with Macbeth again tomorrow but, for now, one of the most famous place-names in Scottish history is just a few minutes drive south of Stirling. The Battle of Bannockburn, 1314, was the decisive battle in the First War of Scottish Independence and saw Robert the Bruce defeat King Edward II of England's vastly numerically superior army to assure Scotland's freedom. The National Trust for Scotland (www.nts.org.uk) has a heritage centre on the site of what is believed to be the location of Robert the Bruce's command post at the Battle of Bannockburn. The impressive statue of The Bruce sat on an armoured horse is the subject of countless photographs. The heritage centre is open from March to October and the grounds are open all year. Check the web site for more details.

If you'd like to go further afield than Stirling and its surrounding area, Scotland's capital city, Edinburgh, is not far to the south. Amongst the city's many fine attractions be sure not to miss the National Museum of Scotland (www.nms.ac.uk) and Edinburgh Castle (www.historic-scotland.gov.uk). The Stone of Destiny, on which Macbeth would have stood or sat when being proclaimed King at Scone, is now at Edinburgh Castle. If you have time whilst in Edinburgh you might also consider a visit to the Scottish National Portrait Gallery where you can see portraits of many famous Scots.

When you have completed your day's activities, return to Stirling where you will stay overnight once again.

Day Seven

Today you will rejoin Macbeth's story as you travel north-east to the locations of some of the decisive events in Macbeth's long reign as King of Alba. Follow local signage in Stirling towards the north-bound M9, which becomes the A9. Travel for about 24½ miles then turn right on to the B934. The village of Forteviot (E3) is about a mile and a half along this road. Now a quiet, pleasant village – rebuilt in the 1920s by John Dewar of the Dewar's Whisky family – within easy commuting distance of Perth, Forteviot was a very significant place in Pictish and later, Alban, times. It was the location of Kenneth MacAlpin's main royal residence and it is said that he died here. It is claimed, also, that a castle or fortification belonging to Malcolm Canmore, Macbeth's killer and successor once stood in the area though its location has been lost.

It would not be surprising if Macbeth himself spent time here. He would have been keen to associate himself with the power and prestige of his illustrious ninth century predecessor and the best way to do so would have been to occupy his residence. There are no standing remains to see here but look around at the landscape and you will see how agriculturally rich the area is; this would have been one of the reasons for Kings of Alba to want to control of it. There are some fragments of medieval masonry in the parish church and the so-called Forteviot Arch, a carved sandstone arch dating from the 9th century and found just to the west of the village, is in the National Museum of Scotland in Edinburgh.

When you are ready, leave Forteviot on the westbound A935 then after half a mile, go right on to the A934. After a further half mile, turn right at the B9112. When you reach Perth, take the A93 then the A94 almost eight miles, passing New Scone on your way to a road on the right signposted for Collace. Travel down this road about a mile and a half.

Just beyond the village of Collace, north of Dunsinane Hill

(E4), there is space to park beside the road. There is an interpretation board here too, a good place to prepare yourself for the walk up Dunsinane Hill. And you will need to prepare yourself because the summit of the hill is 310 metres above you and it is a stiff walk. As you pause for breath on the way, look around you. The view is a spectacular one, the rich farmlands stretching away into the distance. It is clear that a fortification here would dominate the lands for miles around.

Continue all the way to the top of the hill. It is quite flat at the top, the remains of an earlier Iron Age fortification showing only as low mounds around the summit. From the top you can see for miles, making this perhaps the most visually striking of locations you have visited during your exploration of the sites associated with Macbeth. It is easy to imagine Macbeth and his war band atop Dunsinane Hill, fires lit against the cold even in the summer nights, waiting for news of the approach of Malcolm Canmore's forces in July 1054.

As you will see for yourself, your view in all directions from the summit of Dunsinane Hill is a commanding one. You can see the Firth of Tay south of you, for instance, and imagine the sight of Malcolm's forces moving towards the hill. To the north is Birnam Wood, visible across the valley. Shakespeare made Birnam famous and perhaps he was influenced by an earlier folk memory, but we would be surprised if Malcolm's main force approached Dunsinane from the north; a southern approach is more likely, perhaps with Alban forces loyal to Malcolm's family joining from the direction of Birnam Wood. Possibly the approaching spearmen really did make it seem like a forest on the move, and the knowledge that he was losing support from within Alba spelled the beginning of the end for Macbeth.

Did Macbeth and his men wait passively for their enemies to assault the hill, or did they charge down the slope, hoping that the momentum of their charge would dislodge their foes? We do not know, but it is difficult to imagine Macbeth waiting passively for things to happen.

The reality was that despite the strength of the position on Dunsinane Hill, Macbeth was defeated and had to withdraw. He probably left many dead and wounded comrades behind on the hill and on the plain below, but he was forced to retreat in order to try and recover his strength and oppose Malcolm's invasion once more.

The battle over, Macbeth retreating northwards towards his Moray heartland and the cries of the wounded ringing in your ears, return to your car and drive northwards past Collace back on to the A94, turning right to travel eastwards to Coupar Angus. You are heading towards Dunkeld (D2) and our suggested route takes you via 'A' roads. If you prefer you can take a more direct route via minor roads heading generally north-west, but the driving instructions are complicated and we have not included them here.

When you reach Coupar Angus about six miles away, follow local signs for the A923 then, after just over a mile, follow the A984 westwards some 13 miles to Dunkeld. When you get to Dunkeld, follow local signage for car parking. The town is very popular with visitors and car parking is at a premium, so please be patient.

Dunkeld is a very attractive town in a beautiful location so you should not rush your visit to this place. Little of the town you see dates earlier than the 17th century but the settlement is an ancient one. In the ninth century Kenneth MacAlpin had some relics of St Columba brought from Iona, at which time Dunkeld became the ecclesiastical centre for Alba, a status it was to lose in due time to St Andrews.

The cathedral building you see in Dunkeld today is a later medieval construction and there are unfortunately no standing remains of the earlier Christian settlements. But the present ruins are nevertheless deeply evocative and it is easy to imagine a church and associated monastic settlement overseen by Abbot Crinan, father to Duncan I of Alba and implacable enemy of Macbeth.

There is a small museum in the cathedral and the grounds provide ample scope for relaxed discovery and reflection on the differences between this region – home of the so-called 'House of Dunkeld' dynasty and Moray, Macbeth's homeland.

If you still have the appetite for more discoveries, you may want to cross the bridge over the Tay and spend some time in Birnam. There, local signage will direct you to Birnam Wood, a beautiful, atmospheric place where one tree, the Birnam Oak, is believed to be a survivor of the great oak forest made famous by Shakespeare.

Return to Dunkeld where you will spend the night in the very heart of the lands controlled by Macbeth's greatest opponents. Macbeth defeated and killed Duncan I, defeated and killed Duncan's father, Abbot Crinan, but in the end was himself defeated and killed by Duncan's son – Crinan's grandson – Malcolm Canmore. If, like us, your sympathies are with Macbeth, then you will not sleep easy in these lands of his enemies, despite their attractiveness.

Day Eight

In preparing these daily itineraries we have taken you on a generally circular route through Alba. On this final day your journey is a simple one: from Dunkeld back to your starting point of Inverness.

Before setting out, however, you might want to consider adding an extra couple of days to your journey by heading west to explore the tiny island of Iona (F1), a place of unique significance in Scotland's history and the burial place of kings including Macbeth and his stepson and successor, Lulach. While the sacred burial ground may contain the graves of numerous kings and others of importance, there are unfortunately no in situ gravestones to mark the precise burial spots of medieval kings. A fine collection of early gravestones can be seen in the Abbey museum.

We will leave you to plan your own itinerary for Iona but the Iona community web site www.isle-of-iona.com is a good starting point.

But, to return to our proposed final day's journey, the route is direct up the A9, 99 miles from Dunkeld to Inverness. You may want to break your journey by visiting the Highland Folk Museum (http://highlandfolk.museum) which gives a fascinating insight into the more recent (compared to the 11th century at least) history of the Highlands. You will see signposts for the museum mid-way along your journey from Dunkeld to Inverness. Check the museum web site for more information, including opening times, before you set off.

If you decide to visit, don't miss the reconstructed early 18th century township of Baile Gean where costumed guides will introduce you to the way of life of the Highlands at the time of Culloden and the infamous Highland Clearances.

Continue north to Inverness where, if you have time, you might want to visit Culloden Battlefield. The events of April 1745, some 700 years after Macbeth's time, are brought vividly and movingly to life in a newly opened visitor centre and on the battlefield itself where an innovative audio-visual guide tells the story of this iconic event. You will see signposts for Culloden as you near Inverness on the A9.

The final stop on your itinerary brings you back to the story of Macbeth, Mormaer of Moray and King of Alba. Go now to Auldcastle Road, the presumed site of Macbeth's Inverness fortification: you will recall it as one of the first places you visited right at the start of your journey of discovery.

As you stand looking out again over the Moray Firth, just as Macbeth himself must have done, think back over what you have seen as you travelled through 11th century Alba. From this place, Macbeth went on to avenge his father's murder, marry the widowed Gruoch, win the ingship of Alba and defend his hard-won throne until eventual defeat and death at the hand of Malcolm Canmore. We must wonder whether he had any inkling of what the future held, when he stood here where you stand now.

Macbeth, King of Alba, bids you farewell.

Rooted in Scotland

Cameron Taylor
ISBN 1 905222 89 0 PBK £7.99

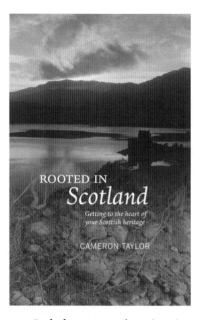

The idea of home can be associated with the notion of an ancestral homeland, a place where something greater than any one individual began. It is difficult to underestimate just how powerful an experience visiting an ancestral homeland can be.

CAMERON TAYLOR

There are several good guides to tracing your Scottish ancestry and many serious historical studies of emigration. *Rooted in Scotland* takes a different perspective. Its starting point is that your sense of connection with Scotland has meaning and legitimacy, and that the journey of discovery that is ancestral research helps you understand who you really are.

Whether you live in the US, Canada, New Zealand or Australia, your Scottish ancestry is worth exploring and celebrating. This book will help you do both.

- The best places to start, tips on exploring your ancestry and a guide to the best websites;

- Includes one man's emigration diary – a one hundred year old first-hand account of what your own ancestors may have gone through;

- Written by an ancestral research expert.

On the Trail of Scotland's History

David R. Ross
ISBN 1 905222 85 8 PBK £7.99

Popular historian David R. Ross tracks Scotland through the ages, detailing incidents, places and people that are key to Scotland's history, from the Dark Ages to Devolution. Leading his readers to ancient monuments and the stories surrounding them, to modern cities and the burial sites of kings, Ross guides us on a quest to discover the essentials of Scottish history – and to find things we never knew existed.

From William Wallace's possible steps, the legend of King Arthur and the reign of Robert the Bruce, to rugged raging battlegrounds, moors and mountains, and Scottish film locations, Ross's journey around Scotland links the past to the present, bringing us face-to-face with the elements that have created the Scotland of today.

An essential read for those who are passionate about Scotland and its mysterious and beautiful tapestry of history and landscape.

The biker-historian's unique combination of unabashed romanticism and easy irreverence make him the ideal guide to historical subjects all too easily swallowed up in maudlin sentiment or 'demythologized' by the academic studies.
THE SCOTSMAN

... an entertainingly outspoken companion for any inquisitive traveller round this nation.
THE HERALD

On the Trail of the Holy Grail

Stuart McHardy
ISBN 1 905222 53 X PBK £7.99

New theories appear and old ideas are re-configured as this remarkable story continues to fascinate and enthral.

Scholars have long known that the *Grail* is essentially legendary, a mystic symbol forever sought by those seeking Enlightenment, a quest in which the search is as important as the result. Time and again it has been said that the *Grail* is a construct of mystical Christian ideas and motifs from the ancient oral tradition of the Celtic-speaking peoples of Britain. There is much to commend this view, but now, drawing on decades of research in his native Scotland, in a major new contribution to the *Grail* legend, the field historian and folklorist Stuart McHardy traces the origin of the idea of fertility and regeneration back beyond the time of the Celtic warrior tribes of Britain to a truly ancient, physical source.

A physical source as dynamic and awesome today as it was in prehistory when humans first encountered it and began to weave the myths that grew into the Legend of the *Holy Grail.*

... a refreshingly different approach to the origin of the Grail.
NOTHERN EARTH

On the Trail of William Shakespeare

Keith Cheetham

ISBN 1 905222 96 3 PBK £6.99

 *On the Trail of William Shakespeare* is Keith Cheetham's latest offering in the series that explores the buildings and locations associated with some of the great figures of world history.

Here, Cheetham tracks Shakespeare's journey from his early years growing up in sleepy Stratford-upon-Avon to his glory days upon the London stage, and through to his quiet death in the mansion house back in the village where he was born. Along the way he visits many 'Shakespeare Houses'; humble farmsteads, mighty castles, palaces, theatres and churches, giving a range of insights into the Elizabethan mode of life, and the life of the Bard in particular.

On the Trail of Scotland's Myths and Legends

Stuart McHardy

ISBN 1 84282 049 4 PBK £7.99

 A journey through Scotland's past from the earliest times through the medium of the awe-inspiring stories that were at the heart our ancestors' traditions and beliefs.

As the art of storytelling bursts into new flower, many tales are being told again as they once were. As *On the Trail of Scotland's Myths and Legends* unfolds, mythical animals, supernatural beings, heroes, giants and goddesses come alive and walk Scotland's rich landscape as they did in the time of the Scots, Gaelic and Norse speakers of the past.

Visiting over 170 sites across Scotland, Stuart McHardy traces the lore of our ancestors, connecting ancient beliefs with traditions still alive today. Presenting a new picture of who the Scots are and where they have come from, this book provides an insight into a unique tradition of myth, legend and folklore that has marked the language and landscape of Scotland.

This is a revised and updated edition of Stuart McHardy's popular *Highland Myths and Legends*.

This remains an entertaining record of the extent to which history is memorialised in the landscape.

THE SCOTSMAN

On The Trail of John Wesley

Keith Cheetham

ISBN 1 84282 023 0 PBK £7.99

 John Wesley (1703–91) founded the Methodist movement, initially an offshoot of the Church of England, which grew into a major church in its own right. In doing so Wesley brought about the greatest religious revival of the 18th century.

The name Methodism derives from the methodical approach Wesley adopted from the Bible for developing personal devotion. His decision to employ lay preachers and preach outdoor sermons on the Word of God to a mainly working-class population angered the Church of England. It led to a split and in 1795, after John Wesley's death, the Methodist Church was established.

Wesley traveled over 250,000 miles across Britain, mainly on horseback, preaching over 40,000 sermons during his lifetime, often facing fierce opposition and persecution. He also spent two years in Georgia, USA, and was author and publisher of much religious material. His work and preaching was known to every branch of society.

On the Trail of John Wesley is a thorough guide to the life and places connected with a man whose work and religious achievements changed the religious face of Britain and established a worldwide Methodist Church.

As well as being a biography, the book is a guide to over 200 Methodist-related sites in both Britain and America.
EXPRESS & STAR (WEST MIDLANDS)

On the Trail of the Pilgrim Fathers

Keith Cheetham

ISBN 0 946487 83 9 PBK £7.99

 The fascinating, true story of the founding fathers of the United States, their origins in England and their harrowing journey to a New World.

After harvest time in 1621 around 60 men, women and children held a great feast in gratitude to God to celebrate their deliverance and the first anniversary of their leaving England to found a settlement in North America. These people became known as the Pilgrim Fathers. The feast was repeated annually and became known as Thanksgiving. Almost 400 years later, US citizens still celebrate Thanksgiving. But who were the Pilgrim Fathers?

In this account, Keith Cheetham tells of their flight to Holland, their subsequent departure from Plymouth on the *Mayflower* in September 1620 and the perils that faced them in the New World. These are true stories of tragedy and danger as well as success.

(This) is a dramatic tale of courage, religious devotion, determination and strength of purpose. It is also one of great sadness, deprivation and hardship.

(Cheetham) has written it partly as a guide-book for those keen to tread in the footsteps of the pilgrims.
EXPRESS & STAR

On the Trail of Queen Victoria in the Highlands

Ian R. Mitchell
ISBN 0 946487 79 0 PBK £7.99

How many Munros did Queen Victoria bag?

What 'essential services' did John Brown perform for Victoria? (and why was Albert always tired?)

How many horses (to the nearest hundred) were needed to undertake a Royal Tour?

What happens when you send a Marxist on the tracks of Queen Victoria in the Highlands? – You get a book somewhat more interesting than the usual run of the mill royalist biographies!

Ian R. Mitchell took up the challenge of attempting to write with critical empathy on the peregrinations of Vikki Regina in the Highlands, and about her residence at Balmoral, through which a neo-feudal fairyland was created on Upper Deeside. The expeditions, social rituals and iconography of that world are explored and exploded from within, in what Mitchell terms a Bolshevisation of Balmorality. He follows in Victoria's footsteps throughout the Cairngorms and beyond, to the further reaches of the Highlands. On this journey, a grudging respect and even affection for Vikki ('the best of the bunch') emerges.

On the Trail of Bonnie Prince Charlie

David R. Ross
ISBN 0 946487 68 5 PBK £7.99

On the Trail of Bonnie Prince Charlie is the story of the Young Pretender. Born in Italy, grandson of James VII, at a time when the German house of Hanover was on the throne, his father was regarded by many as the rightful king. Bonnie Prince Charlie's campaign to retake the throne in his father's name changed the fate of Scotland. The Jacobite movement was responsible for the '45 Uprising, one of the most decisive times in Scottish history. The suffering following the battle of Culloden in 1746 still evokes emotion. Charles' own journey immediately after Culloden is well known: hiding in the heather, escaping to Skye with Flora MacDonald. Little is known of his return to London in 1750 incognito, where he converted to Protestantism (he reconverted to Catholicism before he died and is buried in the Vatican). He was often unwelcome in Europe after the failure of the uprising and came to hate any mention of Scotland and his lost chance.

Yet again popular historian David R. Ross brings his own style to one of Scotland's most famous figures. Bonnie Prince Charlie is part of the folklore of Scotland. He brings forth feelings of antagonism from some and romanticism from others, but all agree on his legal right to the throne.

Ross writes with an immediacy, a dynamism, that makes his subjects come alive on the page.
DUNDEE COURIER

On the Trail of John Muir

Cherry Good

ISBN 0 946487 62 6 PBK £7.99

Only by going in silence, without baggage, can one truly get into the heart of the wilderness. All other travel is mere dust and hotels and baggage and chatter.
JOHN MUIR

Follow the man who made the US go green. Confidante of presidents, father of the American national park system, trailblazer of world conservation and voted a Man of the Millennium, John Muir's life and work is of continuing relevance. He was a man ahead of his time who saw the wilderness he loved threatened by industrialisation, and determined to protect it, a crusade in which he was largely successful. His love of the wilderness began at an early age and he was filled with wanderlust all his life.

Braving mosquitoes and black bears Cherry Good set herself on the trail – Dunbar, Scotland; Fountain Lake and Hickory Hill, Wisconsin; Yosemite Valley and the Sierra Nevada, California; the Grand Canyon, Arizona, Alaska; and Canada – to tell his story.

Muir's importance has long been acknowledged in the US with around 200 sites of scenic beauty named after him. He was a Founder of The Sierra Club which now has over half a million members. Due to the movement he started, some 360 million acres of wilderness are now protected. This is a book that shows John Muir not simply as a hero but as a likeable, humorous and self-effacing man of extraordinary vision.

On The Trail of Robert the Bruce

David R. Ross

ISBN 0 946487 52 9 PBK £7.99

This book from Scots historian David R. Ross charts the story of Scotland's hero-king from his boyhood, through his days of indecision as Scotland suffered under the English yoke, to his assumption of the crown exactly six months after the death of William Wallace. Here is the astonishing blow by blow account of how, against fearful odds, Bruce led the Scots to win their greatest ever victory. Bannockburn was not the end of the story. The war against English oppression lasted another 14 years. Bruce lived just long enough to see his dreams of an independent Scotland come to fruition in 1328 with the signing of the Treaty of Edinburgh. The trail takes us to Bruce sites in Scotland, many of the little known and forgotten battle sites in northern England, and as far afield as the Bruce monuments in Andalusia and Jerusalem.

On the Trail of Robert the Bruce is not all blood and gore. It brings out the love and laughter, pain and passion of one of the great eras of Scottish history. Read it and you will understand why David R. Ross has never knowingly killed a spider in his life. Once again, he proves himself a master of the popular brand of hands-on history that made *On the Trail of William Wallace* so popular.

On the Trail of Robert the Bruce *follows the turbulent fortunes of the 'comeback king' (...) while presenting many unexpected twists in one of the great Scottish legends. Ross has a determination to reach out and bring history*

Luath Press Limited

committed to publishing well written books worth reading

LUATH PRESS takes its name from Robert Burns, whose little collie Luath (*Gael.,* swift or nimble) tripped up Jean Armour at a wedding and gave him the chance to speak to the woman who was to be his wife and the abiding love of his life. Burns called one of 'The Twa Dogs' Luath after Cuchullin's hunting dog in Ossian's *Fingal*. Luath Press was established in 1981 in the heart of Burns country, and is now based a few steps up the road from Burns' first lodgings on Edinburgh's Royal Mile.

Luath offers you distinctive writing with a hint of unexpected pleasures.

Most bookshops in the UK, the US, Canada, Australia, New Zealand and parts of Europe either carry our books in stock or can order them for you. To order direct from us, please send a £sterling cheque, postal order, international money order or your credit card details (number, address of cardholder and expiry date) to us at the address below. Please add post and packing as follows: UK – £1.00 per delivery address; overseas surface mail – £2.50 per delivery address; overseas airmail – £3.50 for the first book to each delivery address, plus £1.00 for each additional book by airmail to the same address. If your order is a gift, we will happily enclose your card or message at no extra charge.

Luath Press Limited
543/2 Castlehill
The Royal Mile
Edinburgh EH1 2ND
Scotland
Telephone: 0131 225 4326 (24 hours)
Fax: 0131 225 4324
email: sales@luath.co.uk
Website: www.luath.co.uk